COMPARATIVE EDUCATION

COMPARATIVE EDUCATION

Edited By
Vijaya Kumari Kaushik
S.R. Sharma

ANMOL PUBLICATIONS PVT. LTD.
NEW DELHI - 110 002 (INDIA)

ANMOL PUBLICATIONS PVT. LTD.
H.O.: 4374/4B, Ansari Road, Darya Ganj,
New Delhi-110 002 (India)
Ph.: 23261597, 23278000

B.O.: No. 1015, Ist Main Road, BSK IIIrd Stage
IIIrd Phase, IIIrd Block,
Bangalore - 560 085 (India)
Visit us at: www.anmolpublications.com

Comparative Education

Reprint, 2006
Reprint, 2008

PRINTED IN INDIA

Printed at Mehra Offset Press, Delhi.

Contents

Preface

'Comparative' techniques paves the way for improvement and development in Education system of one nation. Of late this has become more popular.

In the present book an endeavour is made to analyse and interpret fundamental issues of comparative education.

The rich contents viz., Introduction: Comparative education systems; Indian education; Education in France; California education in America; Education in Malaysia; Education in Latin America; Education in Thailand; Education in Japan; etc., would prove of utmost use for students, teachers and policy planners.

—**Editors**

1

Introduction : Comparative Education Systems

To attempt to carve lessons from past developments in higher education in different countries is a risky undertaking. A system of higher education is not merely a set of institutions which some young people enter and from which fewer later emerge armed with a sheepskin. As higher education has increasingly become the chief, if not almost exclusive, channel for upward mobility, it increasingly determines who will be a nation's elite and what their social roles are likely to be. It incorporates the values and visions of the society of which it is a part and is rooted in a nation's history and priorities. The notion that the systems of higher education of different countries might learn from each other must take this into account.

Even though a country cannot solve its problems by borrowing directly from the experience of others, it can perhaps benefit from seeing them in a wider frame of reference than mere self-examination permits. It is therefore useful to examine the different approaches to common problems in higher education. I shall discuss the following common problems facing higher education in the 1970s: soaring enrollments and costs, the need to diversity and yet co-ordinate higher educational institutions, finding the right balance between co-ordination and institutional autonomy and, within institutions, between professional power and other power, and finally devising a comprehensive and reliable methodology for planning which will in fact be used in making policy.

Increased Enrollment and Rising Cost

The principal immediate problem is expanding enrollments. On a worldwide basis enrollments in higher education almost tripled between 1950 and 1965. In the 22 member countries of the Organization for Economic Co-operation and Development (OECD), comprising most of Western Europe, the United States, Canada, and Japan, enrollments went up in the same period from nearly four million to close to ten million, or by 250 percent. By 1980 another 12 million students may be enrolled in higher education in those countries. In India enrollments have increased eight-fold since 1950.

A major OECD target in the 1960s was to reduce the inequality of access to higher education among different levels of society. This was not achieved. Youth from upper strata still make up about one-third of all students in higher education in the OECD countries. The proportion of students from the lower and middle social strata failed to go up. Nevertheless, in terms of absolute numbers, this latter group more than doubled. Higher education is thus having to adjust to two pressures: an enormous increase in student numbers and a major increase in students coming from different backgrounds and having different expectations and demands than the students traditionally served by the higher education institutions in Western Europe and elsewhere.

Current trends toward more flexible admission to higher education and toward comprehensive secondary schooling will add to the demand for learning from lower socio-economic groups in the 1970s and further diversify the student mix. So will the rising enrollment of women in higher education.

Finally, while past and expected enrollment increases in Western Europe and worldwide are dramatic, the average percentage of 20-24 year olds enrolled in higher education in Western Europe in 1965 was still less than 15 percent. In India it was closer to 3 percent. If higher education institutions ever accommodate the majority of young, people—and the United States is the closest to this with over 40 percent enrolled—radical change will be required in order to cope with such "mass higher education."

Now as to costs. Spiralling enrollments in higher education have been accompanied by proliferating costs. In nearly every country expenditures have been going up much faster than enrollments. In Great Britain, the increase in recurrent expenditures on the universities from 1950 to 1970 was three times the increase in enrollments. In Canada such expenditures have risen more than twelve-fold since 1955. Similar rises have occurred elsewhere. The cost per student has escalated, for example quadrupling for French university students between 1955 and 1965.

Rising costs are prompting measures to retard their rate of increase, and these measures in turn affect the internal functioning and external relations of institutions of higher education. The number of students per teaching staff has risen. Staff-student ratios are as high as 1:40 and even 1:60 in some European university faculties or departments. The proportion of junior and part-time teaching staff to total staff has gone up sharply in all the continental European countries. In a shortage period they are more available and less expensive. They are also increasingly demanding a part in decision-making more commensurate with their contribution to teaching.

Economy measures aimed at restricting the demand on higher education resources are altering the composition of student bodies. To maintain some balance between student numbers and available laboratory and other facilities, especially in science courses, the German universities have introduced a system of quotas or *numerous clauses* on admissions. The "closed" faculties of the Swedish universities have comparable entry restrictions. Throughout Western Europe enrollment increases have been most pronounced in the social sciences and humanities. One can speculate that the rapid expansion in these relatively less expensive fields, a by-product of the financial squeeze on higher education, has had its impact on reform in internal governance, as it is the students enrolled in these fields who have spearheaded demands for wider participation in governance.

Other economy measures may have had an opposite impact. France, Sweden and Germany have taken steps to shorten the study period required to obtain a first degree and are simplifying requirements for advanced degrees. Everywhere, university systems plagued by high drop-out rates are seeking to reduce them and to eliminate so-called "perennial students." These and other measures aim at increasing the productivity of higher education and diminishing pressures on sorely taxed resources. They also leave students less time to press for institutional change.

Rising costs are bringing changes externally as well as internally in higher education. For example, in Great Britain the universities' influence on government decisions with respect to public funding of the universities has diminished. Until a decade ago the universities jointly presented their needs for funds to the government through the University Grants Committee and typically got that they requested. Advisor to government since its establishment in 1919, the University Grants Committee (UGC) represented to government the interests of the universities, serving as a buffer between the dons and government. In recent years the role of the University Grants Committee has become less unilateral. To help assure the universities of the funds they need, it now presses them to rationalize what they do. It is more active in telling the universities what in its view (and that of the government) would best respond to national needs. It suggests which universities should teach in fields where limited student demand and expensive resources indicate consolidation. The UGC also has pressed the universities to analyze how teaching staff allocate their time so that the universities can better justify and even improve their utilization of costly teaching resources. In short, the pressure of rising costs has gradually transformed the University Grants Committee from an instrument largely of one-way communication and a means of warding off government into a two-way medium.

Perhaps the most dramatic new international development in higher education, aimed at least in part at reducing costs, is the establishment or expansion of non-university higher education: The University Institutes of Technology (IUT) in France; the polytechnics in Great Britain; the community colleges, Colleges d'Enseignement General et Professionals (CEGEP), and the Colleges of Applied Arts and Technology (CAAT) in Canada; the Engineer Schools in the Federal Republic of Germany; and on the other side of the world the Colleges of Advanced Education (CAE) in Australia and higher technical schools in Japan. The establishment of university branches or affiliated universities by four universities in Sweden appears to be part of the same pattern.

These new kinds of higher education institutions date with few exceptions from the 1960s. Their costs per student are or are alleged to be less than the universities'. They tend to have less stringent admissions requirements than the universities and therefore provide more democratic access. These new and growing institutions claim to offer programs geared more to the application than discovery of knowledge and to be more oriented toward the student with practical aptitudes—the future technician and junior executive. It is consequently alleged that these new institutions are more responsive to meeting national demands for trained manpower. At the same time at least some of them seem to follow university models to enlarge their offerings in general education, to complete in part for the same faculty as universities, and even, in the case of Britain and Australia, to offer awards having equal status with university degrees. And like the universities, these new institutions are developing, not in isolation, but co-ordinated among themselves and part of the total higher education system.

Problems of Co-ordination

If soaring enrollments and costs are critical problems common to virtually all systems of higher education today, co-ordination may be a yet more difficult problem. A look at the new polytechnics in Great Britain illustrates the complexities.

The polytechnics offer professionally oriented programs of university and subuniversity level to part-time and full-time students and focus on teaching rather than research. Their admissions requirements are less rigorous than the universities. The "poly's" are financed by local governments. However, as more than half of the funds available to the local authorities come from the national government, the polytechnics' level of funding is determined nationally at least indirectly, as well as locally. They are said to be different from the inferior to the universities, although their less rigorous admissions policies and lower levels for faculty salaries, library materials, and student facilities make this open to question.

National policy in Great Britain since the early 1960s has supported the principle that higher education should be available to all who are qualified and wish to attempt it. Carrying out the policy requires decisions on how much and how quickly the three different sectors in British higher education will grow: the universities; the colleges of education which train teachers; and the polytechnics and other post-secondary institutions falling in the so-called further education sector. In the last ten years over half of all students in higher education have been in the universities. If this proportion is to continue and the two-fold rise in enrollment demand anticipated by 1980 is to be met, the universities will need to double their capacity. Otherwise the other two sectors will have to increase proportionately. However, such expansion of the colleges of education is unlikely unless their educational mandate includes more occupations than teaching.

The universities can decide how they will use their resources and what their functions are within the limits of funds allotted for five-year periods by the national government and of the recommendations on academic programs, enrollments, and units costs set forth by the University Grants Committee. In principle they are autonomous. The polytechnics and colleges of education must work within different constraints. The national government sets policy on their functions within the entire system. However, their resources are fixed through negotiation with the local authorities to whom they are in the first instance answerable, and in these negotiations some institutions fare better than others. The expectation that polytechnics and colleges of education will respond to national policy on their role, when decisions are made locally on their funding and functions, result in a peculiar institutional schizophrenia, not to say confusion.

The universities are co-ordinated not only through the UGC but also through their own increasingly vigorous efforts to present a united front to the government and UGC through the Committee of Vice-Chancellors and Principals. This body has become more active in the last few years in formulating and pressing the universities' interests, although interuniversity competition is far from dead. Institutions of advanced further education, including the polytechnics and the colleges of education, are less organized to identify and press for their shared interests vis-a-vis the national government.

This review of the situation in Great Britain suggests some of the problems involved in expanding higher education in an interrelated but only partly co-ordinated system. In education there are no islands. Decisions in one sector and at once level have repercussions at the others. Policy-making at the national level must somehow mesh the national interests in all higher education with the need for some institutions to be particularly responsive to local or regional interests. In such decision-making a balance must be struck among the needs for co-ordination of all higher education, diversity among institutions to meet national, local, and educational interests, autonomy at the institutional level, and equality among different kinds of institutions.

Great Britain is only one example of the problem of co-ordinating the interests that clamor to be heard in determining the future of a national system of higher education. A comparable problem exists in the federally organized countries of Canada and the Federal Republic of Germany, where the constitution places education under the jurisdiction of the provinces and Lander (state governments) respectively. In both countries higher education has become too important or too expensive to leave wholly to these political units.

To help the provinces meet the rising costs of post-secondary education in Canada, the federal government has since 1967 transferred unconditionally to the provinces certain fiscal resources on the basis of a fixed amount per capita for the population of the province or half of eligible operating costs, whichever is higher. This system is a purely fiscal arrangement rather than actual cost-sharing between the federal and provincial governments. The funding and functions of higher education systems in the individual provinces now are determined by the interaction of provincial governments and their higher education systems. The national government can, however, exert influence through its funding of research, student scholarships, and determination of policies on overall national economic development. It may also decide to reduce the extent to which it supports operating costs and may well do so if these continue to soar.

The present arrangement in Canada is somewhat criticized for failing to plan the development of higher education in relation to total national needs. It is questioned most formaking higher education policy so dependent on the provincial governments, some of which are less generous than others and some of which are more interfering than others. The co-ordinating systems that have evolved within most of the provinces represent government to the educational institutions more than vice-versa. Co-ordination on a national basis among the institutions themselves remains limited. After all, the chief target for interuniversity coordination under the present system is the provincial governments, not national government. By the same token intraprovincial co-ordination has developed with considerable vigor in the last decade.

In the Federal Republic of Germany higher education has traditionally been under the Lander and mostly funded by them. However, the federal government for some time has provided funds for research and for one-half of expenditures on student scholarships; more recently it has paid half of the capital costs to expand existing universities and to start new ones. A recent constitutional amendment now permits the federal government to have a more positive role and it has begun to increase significantly its financial support of higher education. The urgency of expanding it and the uneven resources of the Lander to support it dictate enlarged federal role. Even though proposals looking to the creation of new federal bodies to regulate study reforms and to co-ordinate university growth have been watered down in the face of widespread opposition to such federal encroachment, an expanded federal role seems now inevitable. A major step toward this was the establishment in 1970, by the joint agreement of the federal and Lander governments, of the new Commission for Educational Planning to advise on the future of the entire educational system, including higher education.

Autonomy and Governance

The growing external co-ordination of higher education has effects on the internal structure of institutions. Accompanying the trend toward more national or regional co-ordination is a more recent and on the surface, contradictory, move in the continental European countries to decentralize decision-making within higher education systems. Individual institutions are acquiring a larger voice in their own affairs. Complementing this are widespread reforms to broaden and democratize decision-making bodies within the institutions and to introduce into their day-to-day operations the tools of managerial efficiency.

In France, autonomy and participation are basic to the reforms launched by the 1968 Orientation of Higher Education Act. In their teaching and research programs, in finance, and in internal administration, the universities now theoretically enjoy considerable autonomy, although traditions of dominance by the central ministry may be hard to shed. Greater institutional autonomy is a basic aim of reforms in Spain, Italy and Germany. This devolution of authority to educational institutions parallels a trend toward strengthening government at the regional level, thus modifying the extreme centralization long typical of these countries.

Without major change in the role of professors, more institutional autonomy would be an anachronism in higher education systems where, as in France, Italy, Spain and Germany, the full professor has traditionally reigned virtually unrestrained in internal matters. It is not surprising that the oligarchy of the professors has been a leading target for student revolt. The French universities now have a quadripartite representation of professors, students, administrative personnel, and outside interests. Proposed reforms in Italy, while keeping a dominant role for the professors, would give representation to other interests including the students. Student representation in university bodies has existed since the early 1950s in Sweden; current experiments with participation of students, faculty, and other university staff at the departmental level are expected to lead to a yet more substantial student role in the future.

Authority structures in the German universities are yielding to the demand of junior and middle-level teaching staff for a stay in what goes on (after all the now do most of the teaching), and at some of the universities, notably Frankfurt, Marburg, and the Free University of Berlin, students now have an active share in governance. In Great Britain students have steadily accumulated places on university committees, senates and councils, and enjoy a greater role in governing other higher education institutions as well, especially the polytechnics. In Canada student participation—and that of faculty—in university decision-making has widely increased in the last several years.

Everywhere student power is pressing for and winning at least some voice in higher education affairs, often aided and abetted by the parallel demands of the growing ranks of junior teaching staff. However, almost everywhere students are still excluded from decision-making in matters of finance and staff appointments, the last bastion of professorial power.

The multiplicity of interests brought to bear on higher education, as it has become more expensive and devourse an enlarging share of the national product, and the greater size and complexity of individual institutions require more managerial efficiency in higher education administration. The last few years have brought changes here also. Administrators have longer tenure: deans at the "new" universities in Great Britain, the vice-chancellor at Oxford, rectors at the German universities, the new presidents of French universities. Central administrations, woefully understaffed in many systems in relation to the demands on them, are expanding: in Canada, Great Britain, the Federal Republic of Germany and elsewhere. Executive and policy-making organs which university expansion has rendered unwieldy are being streamlined or replaced by smaller bodies that have more authority to determine policy and supervise its implementation.

I have to far receive efforts to co-ordinate, diversify, decentralize, democratize, and achieve greater administration efficiency in higher education. Mounting enrollments and costs have also prompted intensified planning efforts. So that higher education is not again caught off balance by unanticipated developments, planning is everywhere the touchstone of higher education systems. Ten years ago few countries had official planning bodies for higher education. Now in the OECD countries there are few that do not. However, to date the planners have not engendered much credibility among the policy-makers.

The imperatives of expansion in higher education require more reliable planning and more reliance by the policy-makers on the planners. They also call for answers to such questions as whether expansion in future higher education will be determined by the market situation or by analyses of national need or a combination of both, and how these will be forecast and fed into the policy decisions made. Study of such questions is now gathering momentum. However, in general, planning remains peripheral and inadequate at a time when firm and informed decision are required.

George Santayana wrote that "those who do not learn from history are forced to relive it." What then can be learned from the developments touched upon in this review? I suggest the following hypotheses.

1. The traditional function of higher education—to train the elite for university teaching and research and for the professions—has become obsolete. Today higher education should be available to all qualified young people regardless of background, and to other age groups as well, offering the opportunity for professional mobility, enlarged personal satisfaction, and the knowledge and skills need to function in an increasingly complex environment.

2. Higher education should also provide much of the training and new knowledge that contemporary society requires and should be responsive to changing demands. Converting this mandate to an actually is likely to require more money and planning and most specially a better understanding of higher education so that it can be consciously adapted to new needs.

3. As the expansion of enrollments in higher education does not necessarily increase the proportion of students coming from the middle and lower levels of society, positive

steps must be taken to increase this proportion. Conditions obstructing equal access to higher education need to be better understood.

4. The enlargement of higher educations mandate and the increasing heterogencity of the student population demand diversity within higher education: diversity in programs, approaches, resources, and aims, and from to experiment. Diversity calls for a system of differentiated institutions or of comprehensive institutions incorporating a variety of programs, methods and aims or some combination of these.

5. A pecking order appears to be an endemic affliction, if -not an accountability, in systems of higher education. Elitist traditions continue to give first place to the universities, tempting non-university institutions to approach on university resources and to pirate their aims, thereby eroding distinctions between university and non-university higher education. Stub-as this pattern may be, diversity and equality must be reconciled if a differentiated system enrolling students with diverse aptitudes and aspirations is not to relegate some institutions and their students to an inferior streams.

6. Institutions autonomy must allow wider participation of various interests in the governance of institutions than was permitted by traditional patterns if the institutions are to be responsive to their several constituencies within and without. The trend to include in university governance representatives of the students, junior teaching staff, lay interest groups, and even professors where they were previously excluded from central governing bodies, as in Canada, is a necessary one. It permits a balance between broad participation and professorial prerogative more in keeping with the growing diversity of aims and interests that higher education must now serve. But, because these

aims and interests very among institutions and systems, the circumstances of each should in each case dictate the right balance. No single formula can apply, and the balance must remain precarious.

7. Despite the differences in higher education structures, aims, and problems in different countries, they can in fact learn from each other. How the central grants commission has evolved in one country may be useful to another which follows the same basic model. How Australia is developing mechanisms to reconcile federal and state interests in a national system may enlighten the efforts of each other federal states as Germany and Canada, or vice versa. Costing procedures worked out in one system are relevant to others. As problems of rising enrollments and costs and of devising appropriate structures to co-ordinate growth and decision-making become increasingly severe and typical—more in the developed countries but also in the developing—no higher education system can afford not to examine and profit from the experience of other systems facing comparable challenges.

The Federal Republic of Germany

As the name indicates, the Federal Republic of Germany is in fact a federal state. So we have two kinds of "state": the federal state and the constitutive states, political bodies more or less independent which together make up the federal system. The federal state as well as the individual states naturally have their own governments; one should therefore distinguished between the federal government and the state governments. In what areas the federal authorities should be responsible has been laid down by the federal constitution. It has a clause by which it is made clear that all responsibility rests with the states, if there is no other regulation provided for by the federal constitution itself. When you take into account that there exist 11 states in the Federal Republic of Germany, besides the federal government, you might imagine the difficulties involved in forming national science policy in Germany.

In May 1969 a major change in the federal constitution was agreed upon. Before that time the responsibility for the universities—which, as the bulk of institutions for higher learning and science, shall here stand for the rest of similar organizations in the field—rested exclusively with the states. This responsibility included the appointment of professors and other senior staff members in their capacity as civil servants, as well as the total maintenance of the universities, e.g., the financing of recurrent and non-recurrent expenditures for the staff, building equipment and all other facilities. Now the federal government has the legal power to frame general regulations for the state universities. It is also obligated to pay half of the expenditure for new buildings and the first equipment for these buildings, to participate in the financing of major research programs and has some other rights which will not be dealt with here. The increase of power for the federal authorities will lead to the first direct influence of the federal government in university affairs.

The universities, on the other hand, are protected by the same constitution. It proclaims: "Art and science, research and teaching shall be free." In accordance with this constitutional guarantee our universities enjoy a rather independent legal status despite the fact that they are state universities and practically totally subsidized by money coming from the taxpayer. The limitations set to the functions of the governments with regard to the internal affairs of the universities imply an acknowledgment of and regard for the sphere of academic self-administration. The influence of the governments in this sphere remains restricted to its supervisory role, founded in the respective university laws or university statutes.

The sphere of academic self-administration includes primarily matters of research; issues involving academic teaching, especially the organization of studies with due regard to examination regulations; recommendations for appointments to the teaching staff; the awarding of academic degrees and honors; the formal admission and discharge of students; and the maintenance of order within the university, including disciplinary actions.

So, the relationship between the universities and the governments is marked by a pattern of interaction and interdependence between the governments and the academic self-administration, that is, the administration exercised by the universities themselves. The right division of powers between the government, which provides on the whole all the money for the maintenance of the university, and the university with its independent self-administration emanating from the constitutionally guaranteed academic freedom, poses the problem with which universities and governments have to cope every day.

Regarding the intricate system of responsibilities of the federal and the state governments on one side and the rights of the universities on the other, one might easily come to the conclusion that the mere division of powers will inhibit any real influence, exerted by the universities as such, on the shaping of national policies. And one has to admit indeed that the German universities do not play the role in the process of forming national policies which should be attributed to them by the fact that they have such a tremendous amount of knowledge and know-how at their disposal. The governments, on the other hand, are not able to cope directly with internal university problems.

The State Level

Despite the fact that the major responsibility for the

universities still rests with the state governments, there is little evidence of voluntary close co-operation between the governments and the universities on the state level. Of course, due to the historically overcome and now often legally framed set-up of interactions between the governments and the universities, there always has to be some kind of co-operation, but this is mostly on the administrative side. Although it is not always easy to differentiate between administrative and political aspects of a specific question, it should be fair to say that there was, until recently, hardly any participation of the universities at all in the process of shaping a common policy towards the universities on the state level. One might also say that the state governments themselves did not develop and follow clear-cut policies in this field. Only lately have governments of the major states created advisory councils, mostly through nomination by the minister of education, in which not the universities as such, but individual professors and university administrators are asked to give their opinion and advice to the minister and his administration on specific university matters.

Some co-operation of various degrees exists among the universities of a particular state. The rectors of the universities of the area come together and discuss common problems. They sometimes even form a common policy. Mostly this will be directed to fend off attacks on the universities, but sometimes they also make suggestions for university reform addressed to the government. Recently it has been suggested that university councils be institutionalized by law and provide a broad participation of all groups concerned with university matters, including students to a large percentage. On the other hand, co-operation among universities rarely crosses the borderline between one state and another.

Thus one might say that there exists—besides the effects of student unrest—very little influence of the universities on government decisions at the state level.

The Federal Level

In contrast to that situation one finds a relatively broad, even formalized flux of influence of the universities on government decisions and vice-versa. I am supposed to restrict my remarks to the Science Council (Wissenschaftsrat), but I should like to mention rather briefly two other agencies to give you a relatively clear-cut picture of the educational planning system on the federal in West Germany.

The Science Council consists of 39 members: 11 delegates from the 11 states (10 ministers of education, 1 minister of finance), 6 under-secretaries of state nominated by the federal government; 16 scientists nominated by the three greatest scientific organizations (the German Research Organization, the Max-Planck Society and the West German Rectors Conference) and appointed by the President of the Federal Republic; and 6 more personalities from public life, who are nominated jointly by the federal government and the state governments for appointment by the President of the Federal Republic. The term of non-governmental members of the Council is three years. On the basis of parity in the number of votes, the Science Council is divided into a Scholarly or Scientific Commission (22 members) and an Administrative Commission (17 members, but 22 votes).

Any recommendation given by the Science Council (it does not have executive powers, but only makes recommendations) has to be passed by both commissions in plenary session. At first, members of the Scientific Commission, very often together with representatives from the Administrative Commission and experts from various fields, work in small teams on the particular problems.

Then their proposals are thoroughly discussed, first by the Scientific Commission, afterwards by the Administrative Commission, and are finally presented to the plenary session for acceptance or refusal. A two-thirds majority vote is required on any subject.

The Science Council was set up in 1957 by an agreement between the federal government and the governments of the 11 states. The following responsibilities were assigned to the Science Council; to produce an overall plan for the promotion of the sciences (humanities as well as natural sciences); to work out an annual program of priorities to this end; and to make recommendations for the use of funds allocated in the budgets of the federal government and of the states to support science. So far, the assignment of producing an overall plan for the promotion of science and humanities proved too big to grasp in one attack. The Science Council, therefore, tried to divide the subject into three parts: in 1960 it passed recommendations for the expansion of the university; in 1964 it made recommendations concerning the scientific libraries; and in 1965 its recommendations dealt with research institutions outside of the universities, academies of science, museums and scientific collections. All these recommendations were directed toward improving the personnel and material situation of the institutions in question.

Recommendations for the reform of studies in the universities (1966) and for the improvement of the administrative structure of our universities (1968) were supposed to serve as first steps for the necessary transformation of the German university of the nineteenth century into one of the last third of the twentieth century. A major step in this direction was taken by the Council's recommendations on the expansion and structure of German universities from May 1970 until 1980. This master plan for the development of our universities in the next decade served as a basis for the educational program of the federal government now in power. The master plan for the universities will be followed by a master plan for research in the Federal Republic of Germany covering not only research in the universities, but also in all others fields, including research in government institutes as well as in industry.

I will not address myself to the specific contents of all of these recommendations but to one suggestion made in 1967 for the expansion of research in and outside the universities, the so-called "special research area program" (Program der Sonderforschungsbereiche).

The main goals of this scheme to foster research are on the one hand the creation of research units with the chance of greater scientific success (through institutionalized close co-operation among scholars from universities and other research institutions in the same scientific field), and on the other hand, the concentration of the material and human resources to this end. The German Research Association has been asked to advise the Science Council on the selection of the special research areas and to manage the operation of the program.

While the "standard program" and the "priority program" of the German Research Association deal with the individual scholar and his specific single research project, the special research area program deals with groups of scholars working in broader research areas which already are or will be formally organized to achieve closer co-operation in their scientific area. By this it is believed that the combined and institutionalized scientific efforts, together with the additional money for the various research areas, will result in greater scientific success.

The special research area program is based on close co-operation between the universities which have, as self-administered bodies, to apply for a nomination in the official list of the program which will finally lead to special funding. The German Research Association, with its majority of scientists in the decision-making bodies elected by the universities, has to examine the scientific merits of the applications. And the Science Council with its equal votes in the Scholarly and the Administrative Commissions has to decide whether a specific program should be put on the list or federal and state support or note. Thus the federal government, the state governments, and the universities have to co-operative in formulating this nationwide research program.

Although the Science Council can only make recommendations, the mere fact that ten state ministers of education, one state minister of finance and six under-secretaries from the federal government participate in the preparation and framing of the Council's recommendations ensures that the Council's recommendations will be followed—at least to some extent. This might be proved by the fact that $2 million were provided for this program in the first year, $5 million in 1969, $11 million in 1970 and $26 million in 1971. It is hoped that by the mid-seventies the money available for this project will run up to about $100 million per year.

The rules for this program provide the chance not only for the universities, but also for the federal government, the German Research Association and the Max Planck Society, the greatest research organization outside the universities, to make suggestions for the nomination of special research areas. This means that uncovered areas might be taken into consideration for nomination and funding. Thus, an active science policy will emerge in due course through this program instigating research in areas which are not dealt with as yet. Taking into account the importance of research for such a highly industrialized country as the Federal Republic of Germany, one is inclined to say that this scheme opens new dimensions for the formation of a national science policy.

The outline of the structure, the working process, and the example of the special research area program may give you a certain idea about the Science Council as an instrument in which federal and state governments, together with scientists and people from public life, co-operative to recommended new aspects of science policy. It is up to the governments whether they heed the advice or not.

The same destiny of the Science Council is shared by a similar body, the German Educational Council (Deutscher Bildungsrat). While the task of the Science Council is more or less restricted to the field of science in the German sense of "Wissenschaft" and its institutions, the Educational Council deals with all the other educational matters, especially schools. It also can only make recommendations; and despite the fact that the governments participate in the process of forming these recommendations, it is up to them how far they are inclined to follow them.

Due to this, both Councils strongly emphasized the need for a scheme by which the federal government and the state governments should be more or less forced to take into account the thoroughly worked out advice of the Councils when deciding upon matters dealt with before by these Councils. Taking note of the necessity for, such an instrument, the federal and state governments have agreed to set up a new policy instrument: The Commission for Educational Planning (Bund-Lander-Komission fur Bildungsplanung). Seven ministers from the federal government and one minister from each of the 11 states will decide about the future shape of the German educational system, from kindergarten to post-graduate studies and research.

The major basis for the Commission's decisions will be the recommendations of the Science Council and the Educational Council. Thus, the ring is closing. The new German planning system in educational research, and other scientific matters is taking shape: While the Science Council and the Educational Council furnish recommendations for development in their respective fields, representatives of the federal and state governments use these recommendations of their advisory bodies as bases and tools for their common executive efforts to promote education and science in the Federal Republic of Germany.

Some Problems Facing and Science Council

As in any other country not all things are as clear cut as a speech of a foreigner often seems to indicate. Naturally the Science Council is also facing problems. They show not only the complexity of its task, but also the fact that it is merely a body handing out recommendations which try to influence the development of the field of science. The transfer of recommendations into action is more and more becoming the major problem of the Science Council. As far as the executive branch is concerned, things have improved since the Commission for Educational Planning was set up. There are certainly always major differences cropping up in the Commission which have to be dealt with. But politicians are people to get along with as long as—in Germany—there are no matters of "Weltanschauung" involved. A much harder task is to keep in close contact with the universities, where reform activities have to take place first if one is not satisfied with superficial results to show off with. If a reform of the educational system on that level is really to be successful, things have to come from or go to the roots; the same is true for the recommendations of the Science Council. Things went rather smoothly as long as the West German Rectors Conference—something similar to the British Vice-Chancellors Conference—refrained from acting as a political instrument. Common conferences, participation of members of the West German Rectors Conference in subcommittees of the Science Council proved to be sufficient for achieving the common goal: to improve the situation in and for the universities.

The student unrest also changed the situation in this respect. The West German Rectors Conference is gaining a greater understanding of itself more and more as a political institution, developing its own activities for the renewal of this part of our educational system. Politically staged new university presidents, the participation of representatives from student and other organizations, representing non-professional staff, changed not only the working methods but also the basic relationship with an organization like the Science Council, where independent scientists and ministers of education try to formulate what they think will be the best for the universities. So, there exists a slight—under current circumstances it may be normal—tension between the West German Rectors Conference and the Science Council.

Both sides try to overcome this. A formal agreement has been reached about better information from either organization; regular meetings will serve to calm things down; and a broader participation of members of the West German Rectors Conference in subcommittees of the Science Council will take place.

But a major tool to get through to the universities themselves is something the Science Council developed over the years. Small groups of members of the Council visit all universities in the country, ask more or less nasty questions, and discuss the recommendations of the Science Council with university representatives. This exchange of views helps both partners: the Science Council does not lose contact with the actual problems of the universities and the universities get a chance for firsthand information about what the Science Council tries to achieve by its recommendations.

Finally I should like to mention a problem which has been rather unknown to both Germany and the United States in the past, but which is becoming very important right now. There is no instrument to formulate an overall science policy in the Federal Republic of Germany. Hundreds of institutes, some research organizations, like the Max-Planck Society or the German Research Association, have their ideas about what might be a science policy for their own area. The Federal Ministry of Education and Research runs a number of big science programs. But there is nobody in the position to offer appropriate methods for developing something like an overall science policy. Money will always be scarce and the big question mark is, who is going to tell us where to spend it best? What is best? For the individual, for society, for mankind? I should rather like to add another question: Is it really good—whatever this means—to strive for an overall policy in science and research? I am afraid we have to find out many things before we will be able to answer this question. The only thing I am able to say is that the Science Council will try hard during the next two or three years to find some answers. We would be delighted to exchange our views and ideas with yours, to learn from each other because science and research should not and will not respect national barriers. The development of methods for science policy on the national as well as on the international level is a worthwhile common effort—not least of all to foster good relations in science and research between the United States and the Federal Republic of Germany.

2

Indian Education

Higher education is in a state of crisis. It is almost a universal phenomenon and in India it is no exception. It is a recurrent theme of conferences and committees and world over. To recall one of the latest, there was at Mysore in January 1971 a conference on management and organization of Indian universities. The conference was attended by several vice-chancellors and prominent educationists. It was inaugurated by the Union Minister for Education. A widely shared view at the conference was that Indian higher education, rooted in the colonial past, was totally outmoded and chaotic, wasteful and uncreative. It was apparent that nothing less than a radical reform of the system was called for. What was not apparent was the shape and nature of the reform. What exactly was to be done? Who should do it? What about the resources? Educational reform depends upon as well as contributes to economic growth and social change.

Background to Educational Reform

All are agreed that no matter how large the available resources they would be grossly inadequate for the tasks. But there is wide diversity of views about what could be or should be done with the present—admittedly, very meager—resources. How are the priorities to be assessed between competing claims? How are the resources to be divided between average institutions and those striving for high quality? What is a proper balance between teaching and research? Again, not much is known about forecasting of manpower requirements; or how to influence the career choice of students so as to conform to national needs. More fundamentally, how are the available resources to be distributed between different levels of education—elementary, secondary and higher? These are not easy questions. And the difficulties are multiplied manyfold in India where some 70 percent of the population is still illiterate. The literacy rate has increased over the last 10 years from 24 percent to 29 percent, as shown by the census in 1971. But the increase by five points in the literacy rate is more than offset by the rapid increase in population. The total number of illiterates is larger today than in 1961—larger by nearly 50 million.

For a moment let me refer to the gigantic problem of providing elementary education to the Indian children. There are today more than 50 million more children below the age of ten years than a decade ago. Incidentally, it means tht the average age of the Indian population is decreasing—it has decreased by about 3 years in the last 10 years. India is getting noticeably younger. The problem of rapidly increasing numbers is made worse by a large proportion of dropouts, some 50 percent, in the first four years of elementary school. Such large dropouts prevail in nearly all countries with low literacy rates.

The improvement of primary education, as also the improvement of national productivity and agriculture, depends crucially on promotion of adult education. Progress in programs of family planning also depend on progress in education and eradication of illiteracy. Toward this end the universities and colleges can make a significant contribution. One of the new encouraging factors in Indian higher education is the increasing concern and interest of universities in programs of adult and continuing education. This also serves to bring universities and community closer together.

There is now an increasing awareness in the universities, in the government, and by the public about the urgent and imperative need for educational reform. Even more important is the growing realization that meaningful reforms demand careful thought and preparatory work and time, a certain critical level of resources; and involvement of students, faculty and administration; and above all, zest and dedication. Educational reform in a world of rapid change—in a world powerfully influenced by science and technology—has to be a dynamic and evolving concept. The essential thing is to break away from the rigidity and inflexibility of the existing system and to initiate a spirit of change and experimentation.

In a knowledge-based world, despite local variations, many of the basic issues and problems of education are global in character. In today's situation it is apparent that no country by itself, in isolation from others, can resolve its educational crisis. There is much that countries, irrespective of their stage of economic and educational development, can learn from one another. The developing countries should not be carried away by the educational fashions of the affluent ones. Blind copying or import of foreign patterns of education and educational technology can be suicidal. There is a desperate need for effective international support and co-operation in conducting research in management and organization of higher education assessment of performance, and formulation of goals and priorities. Perhaps nothing more than a small beginning has been made so far.

We may ask what contribution the Indian system of higher education has made or could make to other systems of education. Do the Indian universities have a style and mode, ideals and goals, which in some essential respects are uniquely their own? Are there characteristics of Indian universities which distinguish them from their British ancestors of a hundred years ago? The answer by and large is no. There has been no indigenous development such as, for instance, the Morrill Act of 1862 and the foundation of the land-grant colleges in the United States. The Indian universities have new opportunities as never before. There is the great challenge urging them to play a major role in national development, industrialization and social transformation. We desperately need science and technology to raise productivity, but equally we need to accomplish this without distorting and eroding the spirit of science and the essential human values India has cherished over the ages. It is likely that the universities now subject to great pressures, internal and external, will undergo major mutations and adjustments. Their especial contribution may well be an enlargement and sophistication of Mahatma Gandhi's concept of basic education striving to unite manual work, mental work, and moral values. It is, as it were, a creative synthesis of science and non-violence—of *atom* and Gandhi.

Great universities, some of the greatest in the world, flourished in India in ancient times. The most famous of them was at Nalanda. It was founded shortly after the death of Buddha, and it continued for more than 1,500 years till about the close of the twelfth century when it was destroyed by foreign invaders. In the days of its glory Nalanda had some 10,000 students and 1,500 teachers, a student-staff ratio of 8:1. These great universities were an integral part of India's religious, intellectual, and cultural life. But this cannot be said of the Indian universities of today. These are not the successors of Nalanda and Takshasila. Their roots derive from the London University of the early 1850s, which was essentially an examining body with little concern for teaching and research. The British ancestry of the modern Indian universities is all too visible and dominant even today. For instance, it is only in the past two decades since independence that there has been any noticeable effort to give a proper place to modern Indian languages in the universities. The situation till recently was essentially no different from that described by the British vice-chancellor of the University of Bombay in his annual address in 1871,100 years ago. He observed that of the 5,000 students who took the matriculation examination of the university in the 12 years since its setting up in 1857, only 25 percent were successful. The main cause of failure was inability to qualify in English. Those who failed in the other subjects but qualified in English were very few.

In view of the considerable interest in and importance of the question of medium of education and place of English in the Indian universities, let me quote from the statement adopted at the Vice-Chancellors Conference four years ago. The statement says: "The conference recognized that the change-over in the medium of education (from English to the Indian languages) *if properly carried out* would be a major step toward improvement of higher education and toward strengthening of its roots in our soil. The progaam should be pursued in a sustained and systematic manner... In the program of change-over the importance of English should be fully recognized and adequate arrangements for its study made at the under-graduate level."

A serious deficiency of the present system of higher education is that a vast majority of students, especially those studying science, technology, agriculture, and medicine, get no exposure at all to Indian literature and to Indian philosophic and cultural thought.

Higher Education Today

There are certain things about Indian higher education which strike us immediately. The first is the huge size of the enrollment. The second is the inherent rigidity of the system, the existence of affiliated colleges and external examinations. The third thing I should like to draw attention to is the deliberate effort devoted in recent years to development of quality institutions, such as the universities for agriculture, the Indian Institutes of Technology, and the centers of excellence for science and humanities in the universities.

Let us consider the size of the system. At the time of independence in 1948 there were 20 universities. The number is now 83. These include 14 universities almost entirely devoted to agriculture. Their development has been greatly assisted by the United States. Besides the 83 universities there are some 20 institutions of university status. These include the five Indian Institutes of Technology set up with foreign assistance and providing a splendid example of international co-operation of technical education. The *Vidyapiths* at Ahmedabad and Varanasi founded by Mahatma Gandhi and his close associated, at the height of the non-co-operation movement, to serve as centers of national education, were granted university status in 1963 under the Act of the University Grants Commission. I shall say a few words about the UGC later.

The total enrollment in higher education is nearly three million. It is increasing very rapidly. The growth rate exceeds 10 percent a year. In a single year the increase in enrollment now exceeds the total enrollment in higher education for the United Kingdom. Of the total enrollment of 3 million only about 10 percent is in institutions or departments directly maintained by universities. The vast majority of students attend some 3,500 colleges affiliated with the universities. About one-fourth of the colleges are maintained by the government; the rest are privately managed, receives grants from the state. Less than 5 percent of the total enrollment is in evening colleges and correspondence courses, but this is increasing.

The age of students entering higher education is about 17 years. The school education is generally of 11 years' duration. About 4 percent of the youth enter college. For a person of college age the chance of entering college is ten times than at the time of independence. For a Delhi youth the chance is five times more than the national average—the same would hold more or less for other larger cities. As is to be expected, there is a wide variation between states, and college entry depends much on social status of parents and on caste in some cases.

A little over 10 percent of the total enrollment is in technology, medicine, and agriculture. An overwhelming majority of students study arts and humanities. This is so much easier to provide than applied sciences and medicine. Apart from medicine, technology, and a small number of prestigious institutions, the admissions are non-selective—an open entry, as it were. I mentioned earlier that 4 percent of the relevant age group enter higher education. I should add at this point that a considerable part of what is included in Indian higher education would be a part of secondary education in educationally and industrially advanced countries. It terms of international comparability, the proportion of the relevant age group in higher education in India would be less than 1 percent—one of the lowest in the world—as compared to 30-40 percent for the U.S.A., and about 10 percent for the U.K.

The great upsurge in Indian education in the last 20 years has been impelled by social pressures and rising aspirations. It has brought higher education within reach of people who a generation ago had hardly any access to it. The social benefits of educational expansion with its contribution to mobility and erosion of traditional barriers is no small gain. Sometimes this is not fully appreciated. The explosion of numbers has, on the other hand, adversely affected the general level of academic standards. This seems inevitable. Whereas the enrollment is doubling in less than 10 years, it takes very much longer than ten years to double the number of competent teachers. Further, with expanding enrollments, unless the national economy is developing rapidly, expenditure on higher education per student in terms of real value of money, instead of rising, goes down substantially. This is what is happening in India. The Indian Education Commission in 1882 noted that the cost per student per year in government colleges at that time was about Rs. 350. This in terms of purchasing power would be many times higher than the cost per student today.

The number of women students in Indian higher education has grown at a very fast rate, much more than the growth rate for total enrollment. In 1887 the vice-chancellor of the Calcutta University said at the annual convocation, "Another event has happened which may prove an isolated accident, or may prove the harbinger of an important movement. A young native Christian woman applied to be admitted to our entrance examination." At the beginning of the century the number of women students was less than 500. Today it exceeds 500,000. There is also a women's university in Bombay with an enrollment of 10,000. In the Delhi University, women students form more than 40 percent of the total enrollment.

It may be observed that since the establishment of the universities in India 100 years ago the enrollment has been doubling, on an average, every 10 years or so. The corresponding figure for the United States is about 15 years. These are close to the doubling period for the growth of science and technology, but it is not clear if this is anything more than a mere coincidence.

Obstacles to Innovation

I turn now to the rigidity of the Indian higher education system. Most of the university have a large number of so-called affiliated colleges spread over an area of several thousands of square miles. The University of Calcutta, the largest of the Indian universities has some 200 affiliated colleges and an enrollment of 200,000. There is hardly any interaction between a university and its affiliated colleges. The colleges must teach the curriculum prescribed by the university, but it is the university which conducts examinations and awards degrees. The colleges teach a curriculum in the framing of which they had little participation, and prepare students for an examination which is conducted almost entirely by external teachers. In such a system there is not much room for initiative and innovation. The affiliated colleges in any particular university would, as one would expect, vary widely as regards quality of staff and students, library and laboratory facilities, student amenities, and so on. Yet they must all follow the same curriculum, and their students must all take the same examinations. If it is a question improvement of curriculum, or of examination reform, or anything else, either there must be a simultaneous, a synchronized, change in all the colleges of the university, or there is no change at all. A change at the same time in all the colleges, even if it could be introduced, is almost certain to be frustrating because of the wide diversity in motivation and resources of the colleges. The system of affiliated colleges makes the thing so huge, so inert, that to bring about any noticeable change a nearly infinite amount of effort and initiative would be required. A major reform urgently called for is to devise some mechanism which would liberate outstanding colleges from the rigid uniformity of the present lockstep system. Colleges which have adequate motivation and resources and the right climate should be free to move ahead. This is the concept of the *autonomous college*. The university would exercise a measure of general supervision, but otherwise an autonomous college will be free to prescribe its courses, combinations of subjects, admission of students, and recruitment of staff. The degree would be awarded by the university to which the autonomous college is affiliated. The Education Commission which the Government of India in 1964, and which submitted its report in 1966, strongly recommended the adoption by the universities of the concept of autonomous colleges. A good deal of thought has since been given to it by the University Grants Commission and the universities. Despite serious difficulties it is likely that the scheme of autonomous colleges will be introduced in the near future. This would be a major reform of Indian higher education.

I may perhaps also mention at this point about the structure and governance of universities and colleges. The structure and pattern of university governance is very much reminiscent of what prevailed in the University of London in the early 1850s. These were not the days of glory of the London University. Again, what was perhaps adequate for universities and colleges of small size, teaching a nearly unchanging curriculum, and contributing little to research, has become totally inadequate and irrelevant when student numbers have increased a hundred fold and knowledge has expanded at a fantastic rate. A committee of the University Grants Commission under the chairmanship of the vice-chancellor of the Bombay University, Dr. Gajendragadkar, formerly the Chief Justice of the Indian Supreme Court, is currently examining the entire question of university and college governance as well as the participation of faculty and students in academic affairs and governance.

Advances in Higher Education

I now come to what may be called the quality sector of higher education. The special attention paid in recent years to education for agriculture and technology, and the development of a small number of centers of excellence in universities are important steps of great significance and potentially. There are the five Indian Institutes of Technology set up in the last 15 years. The enrollment in the Institutes of Technology is about 10,000. This is about 10 percent of the total number studying technology in universities and colleges in the country. The agricultural universities, now numbering 12, set up with the co-operation of the United States, give special emphasis to integration of teaching, field work, and research. The first agricultural university was set up in 1960. The agricultural universities have made a notable contribution to improving agricultural productivity.

A special mention should be made of the University Grants Commission's scheme of centers of advanced study in the universities. There are 30 centers, 17 in natural science and 13 in humanities and social sciences. The centers have received valuable assistance from the U.S.S.R. through Unesco.

The expenditure per student in the centers of advanced study is about 10 to 20 times the national average for higher education. As the number of centers is very small, the total expenditure on them is only a small fraction of the total expenditure on higher education.

I may add that at the undergraduate level the cost per student per year in higher education is, for most countries, comparable to the per capita GNP of the country. For India the GNP is about Rs. 500 ($70) a year; and that is comparable to the yearly cost of college education per student. But when it comes to advanced study and research, especially in science and technology, the costs in different countries, developing and advanced, become comparable. This is understandable. It means that a country such as India can only provide a much smaller proportion of institutions of high international quality in relation to its educational system that affluent countries can and do. For the success, at this stage, of the scheme of the centers of advanced study, it seems essential that expenditure on them does not exceed, say, 5 to 20 percent of the total outlay on higher education. In other words, establishing the centers should not mean more than a marginal deprivation of the resources devoted to the bulk of institutions in the country. Further, it is important that there are also other programs for improvement of quality available generally to universities and colleges. Perhaps the most important of such programs we have is that of the science summer institutes organized in co-operation with the National Science Foundation of the U.S.A. The summer institutes are at various levels, from research to undergraduate teaching.

University Grants Commission

Let me say a word about the University Grants Commission set up in 1956 under an Act of Parliament. Under the Indian Constitution education is a State subject—not a Union subject. But the Centre has responsibility for co-ordination and maintenance of standards of higher education, and for promotion of technical education. The University Grants Commission is an autonomous body. It receives its funds from the central government—now about Rs. 300 million a year. The Commission's funds are for development of universities—that is, for casual expenditure generally. The maintenance grants to the universities are provided by the state governments. Under the act the Commission's responsibility covers all sectors of education. In practice, however, the Commission has not been dealing with agriculture and medicine. Agricultural education is looked after by the Indian Council for Agricultural Research set up by the Ministry of Agriculture. The Ministry of Health deals with medical education.

The basic idea governing the working of the University Grants Commission is that developing plans for education and formulation of policy is left to a "judgment by peers." It is a system which enables universities to have an effective share in formulation of major education policies and distribution of funds. The Commission functions through committees—review committees, visiting committees and other special committees—composed largely of university men.

I have given a brief and somewhat cursory description of Indian higher education. I have barely touched upon the most important problem facing us which is to link education with productivity. This is engaging the earnest attention of the universities, the government, and the industry. It was Gandhi's concept of education that it should be work-oriented and directly related to the economic and social goals of the community. Gandhi used to say that for him the touchstone for judging the merit of a proposal or an action was the benefit, however small, it would bring to the lowliest man in the country. For education itself there could be no more noble and meaningful touchstate.

The University Grants Committee is that many people would call a "typically British" institution. They mean that on the face of it, it is illogical, irrational and untidy. The answer is that while it may deserve all those adjectives, the fact is that it works—like a good many other institutions which are called "typically British."

The first point that must be made is this. In Britain we do not have the broad distinction that there is in the United States between private and public universities. We do not have a group of private institutions, like Harvard, Yale, and Princeton, which depend for the bulk of their income on endowments and tuition fees, and then a different and separate group of the great state universities, which depend largely on funds voted to them by their state legislatures. Our universities in Britain—Oxford and Cambridge as well as the newest institutions—are all alike in one respect, however much they may differ in others. They all derive something like 90 percent of their capital budget and 85 percent of their operating budget from the Exchequer, that is to say, from federal funds. Some have more endowments that others; but endowment income and income from tuition fees together make up a tiny percentage of their annual budgets.

The second point I must make follows from the first. You might expect that this dependence on the government for money made the universities dependent on the state in other ways, that they were controlled by the state, and that their academic freedom, as institutions and as individuals, was bound to be limited by this financial and economic fact. One of the main reasons for the existence of the University Grants Committee is precisely to ensure that this does not happen and to protect and preserve the academic freedom of the universities. It stands between the university world and the government, interpreting the one to the other, acting as a buffer between them on the basis that it is trusted by both.

Composition of the Committee

The members of the University Grants Committee—UGC for short—are 20 in number. Only the chairman is full-time; the rest are individuals who give one-fifth of their working time, for a ridiculously small fee, to the work of the UGC. Some of them come from industry or commerce or non-university parts of the educational system. But a clear majority of them are practicing university professors, representing all the main subject fields and, as far as possible, the main geographical areas of the country. They do not, and this is important, represent their particular universities;

but collectively they know intimately, from the other four-fifths of their working time, both the atmosphere of the university world and the likely effects on that world of decision taken by the University Grants Committee. They are, please note, professors, not administrators. No university vice-chancellor or registrar or secretary may be a member. I tell my academic friends that to become a member of the Committee is the kiss of death. In no time they will be made vice-chancellors, and they will have to resign from the Committee.

This majority of professors is really the UGC's great strength. You may think that a dozen professors might have difficulty reaching wise decisions about such worldly matters as university budgets or resolving financial arguments with the government. You might even suspect that they just might show a degree of favor toward an institution in which they happened to be personally interested. Indeed, you might wonder what a professor of logic or of pure mathematics could contribute to these matters at all. Well, I have had a fair amount of experience with boards, councils, commissions, committees, and I can honestly say that I have never known any place where decisions were taken more responsibly or more objectively than round the table of the University Grants Committee. I am not, of course, suggesting that the decision were always right, but they were always as objective and responsible as human decisions can be.

The professors are supplemented by businessmen and by members from other parts of the educational field. But it is vital that the UGC's decisions should be based on judgments of academic values; and those judgments properly come from academics. They are also supported by a small but very high-quality staff of administrators and specialists, like architects and quantity surveyors, who are recruited from the career civil service. Here you might possibly expect to find a governmental check on erratic academics, a sort of planning of watchdogs from the official side to ensure that they did not get out of hand. Certainly, it is extremely valuable to have experienced civil servants bringing their expert knowledge of governmental procedures to the Committee's service. And there is a long and stern tradition that when they join the UGC's office the loyalty of these men and women is totally given to the UGC, whatever, government department they have come from. I have seen some splendid battles between the Committee's civil servants and men who a few months before had been their close colleagues in the Department of Education and Science.

One other possible suspicion must be cleared out of the way. All the members of the UGC are appointed by the Secretary of State for Education and Science; so there could be a suspicion that in some sense or other the appointments were political. I can assure you that this is not so. I myself was appointed by a Conservative government. I served under governments of both parties and under a bewildering succession of ministers and secretaries of state. At no time was the question of my party affiliation ever mentioned—which is just as well, because I do not know what my answer would have been. Similarly, when names were being discussed for appointment to membership of the Committee, at no time was that question raised about them. I simply did not know, looking round the table, to which political party, if any, my colleagues belonged. Still less did any of us out of office when there was a change of government.

Recurrent Grant

Well, so much for the membership of the University Grants Committee. What does it do? Primarily and fundamentally, it distributes among the universities the public funds which the government has agreed to allocate to them. But there is a stage before this. Before it can distribute the money, the UGC has to get it from the government. And that can be the hardest part of the whole operation. Let me try to explain how it works.

For purposes of the operating budget—what we call recurrent grant—the government and the UGC work on the basis of a five-years period. Eighteen months or so before the end of an existing five-year period, the UGC writes to each university and says something like this: Will you please tell us what expenditure you expect to incur in each year of the forthcoming quinquennium? You should state this in terms of (a) your present commitments in, for instance, staff salaries; and (b) new developments you want to start, with estimates of their cost. We want to know, please, in exact detail, how much money all this will cost you in each year of the coming quinquennium, together with all your other annual expenditures on building maintenance, administration, non-academic salaries, the lot. And we should also like to know, please, particulars of your income from all sources other than government grant. When this letter is received in each university, a period of intense (and intensive) activity begins. It is a salutary discipline that once in five years each university should have to stand back from itself, do rigourous self-examination, and decide on its priorities—and then write it all down in intelligible form.

Eventually each university replies, and there follows a short period during which the officers of the UGC and the officers of the 44 universities are in touch with each other to clarify and sort things out. Then, when all is clear, the UGC makes a submission to the government. It does not simply add together the amounts requested by each university and send the total as its submission to the government. Each university, you must remember, has sent in its proposals without knowing what other universities have proposed. So you could get a situation in which each one of three universities within a hundred miles of each other had asked for money for new departments of astrophysics or agricultural economics or Chinese language and literature. Then it becomes the UGC's business to exercise an academic judgment about each of the universities concerned and to decide whether it should ask the government for money to enable one or two or all three of the universities to do one or two or all three of these things. To help it in reaching these difficult decisions it has a whole solar system of expert subcommittees dealing with particular academic fields. Like the Committee itself, subcommittees are composed largely of academics. The subcommittee chairmen are members of the UGC. The UGC makes its decisions based on the expert advice of these subcommittees, and then on a great and famous day once every five years, it sends a bulky submission to the government asking for a total sum for all the universities for each of the next five years. It does not ask for money for each university separately; it asks for a total aggregated sum for them all.

Then the fun really begins. Officials of the UGC sit down with officials of the Department of Education and Science and go through the whole submission page by page and line by line. The primary purpose of this very exhaustive (and sometimes exhausting) exercise is not for the department to make cuts in the Committee's proposals, although that does sometimes happen on the way. The real purpose of these hard-working sessions is that the department's officials should thoroughly understand not only the figures which the Committee has put to them but also all the arguments on which those figures are based. Why, the Committee may be asked, do you want so much money for social science courses when there are already signs of unemployment among social science graduates? Why are you not providing more places for mathematicians? Why do you expect, as your estimates seem to show, that the student population at the universities will increase by this percentage over these five years? Why, in a period of financial stringency, cannot the proportion of teachers to students, the so-called staff/student ratio, be reduced? And so on questions of detail or of principle, of manpower deployment, or of sheet statistics—all of them have to be argued out. Some are matters of predictable trend, some of informed judgment, some of near guess-work. But the primary purpose of all this discussion is that the officials of the department should be completely informed—and, we would hope, completely convinced—about the submission which the UGC is putting forward. Then the officials of the department can go with a clear conscience to the Treasury for the necessary money.

There is, of course, a period of further argument at that stage, but I will not bore you with the details. At the end of it comes the third glorious day, when a statement is made in Parliament giving the figures for recurrent expenditure over each of the forthcoming five years approved by the governmental and submitted to Parliament for sanction. The figure, naturally, is bigger for each year as the five-years period proceeds—normal annual increments in staff salaries would require that, apart altogether from new developments. After a little debate Parliament sanctions these figures. And then, wiping off its brow the sweat caused by these arguments with the government, the UGC turns to its task of dividing among the various universities the total amount it has succeeded in persuading the government to provide.

Distribution of the funds is, of course, extremely difficult. The overriding fact is that the total amount voted by Parliament is probably a good deal less than the aggregate of all the amounts originally asked for by the universities individually. If this were not so there would be no problem. But the distribution has to be done, and always with the knowledge that people are going to be disappointed.

Here again it is one of the Committee's great strengths that it has a majority of academics, as do the subcommittees which again advise the UGC. One of the UGC's continuous activities is visiting the universities. Both its subcommittees and the Committee itself spend a great deal of time talking with the administration, the professors, the non-professional staff, the health service staff, the technicians and, last but by no means least, the students. These visits are not inspections. Nor are they operational occasions when administrative decisions are made. Instead they are opportunities for the Committee to get the feel of each place, and to form qualitative judgments about the people who work in it. This is the background against which the quinquennial distribution is made; and, as I have said, it is a difficult job. Nobody would pretend that every university is satisfied with what it gets. There never is enough money to go round, and I suspect there never will be. But the job is done by a body which knows what it is talking about, knows the university world and knows what will be the effect, in each university, of what the Committee decides.

Block Grant

So each university receives a letter from the UGC telling it its financial fate for each of the next five years. Normally the letter gives some indication of the student numbers, undergraduate and graduate, which the money is expected to provide for. But the crucially important point about the letter is this. You remember that each university was required to give information in the greatest detail about its intended expenditure under each of several relevant headings. When the letter goes from the UGC to the individual universities there is no financial detail and no headings, there is simply a straight total sum for each of the next five years. The original submission from the university was detailed, the allocation to the university is a block grant, with no detail at all. This is an essential and cardinal element in the whole system. It means that inside the total sum the university is free to deploy the money as it chooses. In its own internal annual budget it can decide for itself how much to spend on the library, how many teaching and technical staff to employ, how much to allocate to maintenance of buildings, and so on. This freedom, within the budgetary total, is as nearly complete as any freedom in this world can be, and it is genuinely appreciated by the universities. In a word, the UGC does not run the universities: it tries to provide them with the resources to run themselves.

This block grant principle, as it is called, is vital. Of course a university will have other income which is specifically intended for specific purposes—chiefly research grants from the research councils or from industry—which are made to particular departments or individuals. These are in effect earmarked supplements. The basic recurrent annual grant from the UGC is a block grant for the university to use at its own responsible discretion.

Capital Grant

The procedures for capital grants are quite different. They are not based on a quinquennial system; they are earmarked for a particular building or purchase of land; and they are strictly priced on published standards of cost. But here too the initiative lies with the universities. Each of them tells the UGC the capital expenditure it would like to undertake over the next few years: the UGC argues with the government; the government announces for two or three years ahead how much money it is prepared to ask Parliament to provide; and the UGC has the job of dividing this money among the projects put forward by the individual universities according to its own judgment of their respective needs. Again it is obvious that not everybody will be satisfied—if anybody is—but the decisions have been taken by what is essentially an academic body, the colleagues of those in the universities who are going to be disappointed.

I have concentrated, perhaps too much, on the financial rather than the academic functions of the UGC. But I repeat that the initiatives, all the way through, rest with the universities. They know, individually, what they want to do; and they ask the UGC for the resources to enable them to carry out their ambitions.

Planning and Co-ordination

I said at the beginning that the UGC was a buffer between the government and the university world, standing between them to that there is no direct confrontation of government on the one hand and universities on the other. We believe that this is essential to academic freedom simply because we do not want to see direct influence by the government, any government, on individual universities. Of course, in the end, any government must decide how much money it is going to provide for the universities as a whole in competition with housing, hospitals, roads, defense and all the other claimants on the taxpayer's money. This is a decision on priorities, and such decisions are the proper function of governments. But it is not their proper function to decide how University A shall develop or what studies University B shall encourage or discourage. Hence the original function of the UGC as a buffer.

But a buffer is a pretty passive object, and over the years the UGC has come to behave rather more actively than a well-behaved buffer should. It is now distributing more than £200 million a year, and that is not chicken feed. There are now 44 universities on its grant list, a small number by U.S. standards, but quite a considerable constituency. With the growth in numbers and in expenditure, something like a central strategy is necessary. It no longer makes sense, if it ever did, that every university should try to do everything. There simply are not enough top-class academics available to staff medical schools or schools of nuclear physics or department of agriculture, or schools of Oriental languages in each one of 44 separate institutions; so it must be recognized that different universities will be centers of excellence in different fields. This demands at least the outline of a strategic plan, and it has fallen to the UGC to provide it. This is a heavy responsibility; but, again, the decisions are taken by academics for academics. And as the UGC finds itself encouraging this or discouraging that, at least most academics prefer the judgment of their peers and colleagues to instructions from a government department.

I am not, of course, suggesting that the system is perfect. There are practical difficulties which it does not wholly meet. For example, when there is serious inflation during a quinquennium, the annual block grants dwindle in real value as time goes on; there is no automatic adjustment, and although there are various alleviations and palliatives this is a real problem. Then there is, admittedly, a lack of complete co-ordination between the capital building program and the annual recurrent grant. It can be argued with some force that the development of any university is conditioned by the buildings it can have, and that the operational budget is, in principle, deductible from this. I am not sure that I entirely accept this proposition, but I do accept that there is something to it.

Again, more generally, there is the difficulty of keeping in properly close touch with each separate university and with the Committee of Vice-Chancellors and Principals. The chairman has continuous correspondence and conversation with the vice-chancellors individually, normally on first-name terms, and the officers of the UGC are in almost daily touch with their opposite numbers in the universities. As for the Vice-Chancellors' Committee, the chairman of it and the chairman of the UGC meet for a working dinner at least once a month, and it is normal that a policy statement to be issued by either is shown to the other in draft beforehand for information and comment. But it is true that as the UGC becomes less like a buffer and more like a strategic planning unit and as the Committee of Vice-Chancellors and Principals itself becomes less like a luncheon club and more like the official collective voice of the university, collaboration between the two bodies becomes increasingly important to the success of the system.

More fundamentally, can the UGC guarantee that it is not subjected to political or governmental pressure? I have tried to give reasons why I think it is not: but I cannot prove it in a court of law.

Perhaps this gets us down to the basic facts of life. The whole operation of the University Grants Committee depends on reciprocal confidence between the three partners involved, the universities, the government and the UGC itself. If either the universities or the government ceased to trust the UGCD, the whole gossamer web of this "typically British" institution would collapse.

In my days at the UGC we used to say, among ourselves, that we operated on the Principle of Equal and Opposite Unpopularity. If we were, by any chance, popular with the government, the universities would think that we were in the pocket of the government: if we were, by any chance, popular with the universities, the government would think that we were in the pocket of the universities. In real life there was no danger of either of these positions—we were equally and oppositely unpopular with both. And, if I may presume to say so, I think that in all the circumstances this amounts to a vote of confidence from both.

3

Education in France

Since the student uprisings of 1968, and partially because of them, the French university has gone through a period of profound change. These changes have created a need for co-ordinating the activities of the universities and the policies which the Minister of National Education develops in the name of the government.

The system which existed before 1968 can be easily described. The Minister of National Education. Grand Master of the University and the Rector of each of the 23 academies or Regional Education Authorities presided over the activities of the university.

For each academy, or educational district, there was one and only one university and it was exactly identical to the other universities. Each was composed of five faculties which grouped together the teaching facilities of the same disciplines: law and economics, arts and humanities, physical sciences, medicine and pharmacy. The university as such was not a living organism but a collection of teaching faculties only vaguely related to each other. They were linked directly to the Ministry of National Education by the rector of the academy who was appointed by the government and who was automatically president of the university council.

The options as to the type of education offered in the system were limited. The minister determined the content of courses with the help of several committees composed of professors and specialists. These defined programs and curricula leading to a strictly limited number of degrees at the bachelor's master's or doctoral level. The degrees had the advantage of all being equal in the value in the types of the law.

In short, the uniformity of the texts, of the procedures, of the customs, and of the activities of the university was the rule. However, it must be admitted that behind this official uniformity appeared certain aspects of inequality and originality. For example, it is well known that between the enormous University of Parts—with its 160,000 students and its distinguished professors—and certain small young universities in the provinces, there was considerable difference in the quality of education offered. The problems of the universities themselves were different in intensity, and the lack of power to solve these problems did not always show itself in the same way. Thus, uniformity and centralization of decisions had a tendency to disappear.

May 1968 was a true catalyzer. The law reorganizing university education was passed unanimously on November 12, 1968 by a parliament which finally discovered what a university was and then gave it the legal means to start a transformation. This transformation, which involved the creation of new structures and organisms of decision-making, has now reached the completion of its first stage.

The effect of these changes has been a destroy once and for all the centralized uniformity of the pre-1968 system. What has resulted, of course, it is need for co-ordination of the activities of the numerous bodies concerned with university education.

Need for Co-ordination

The number of universities in France increased overnight

from 23 to 67. The monolithic University of Paris was divided into 13 autonomous teaching institutions. Now, the basic units of the University are no longer the traditional faculties but rather some 700 Teaching and Research Units. Each of these units groups together about 1,000 students and consequently is of a size which should make good administration easier.

The autonomy of the universities now allows them to determine, by means of their elected councils, their teaching activities and their composition. The number and type of Teaching and Research Units will be the main determinant of this last aspect. These units will vary as to their scientific disciplines, their academic level or their teaching activities.

The newly established decision-making bodies were used for the first time in 1971. Each Teaching and Research Unit elected a council composed of representatives of the teaching staff, the student body, and administrative personnel. These councils in turn sent representatives to the larger university council, which for the first time has a number of members drawn from outside the university community. It is this university council from which come the decisions on teaching policy and methods. It also co-ordinates the activities of the various Teaching and Research Units and divides the available financial resources among them.

Each of these councils elects its own president. The rector, chancellor of the university, is still appointed by the government, which he represents. Automatically a member of the university council, he is no longer its president. The role of the rector has not, however, diminished notably: he is still responsible for coordinating university education with primary and secondary instruction and for carrying out the financial policies which are given film by the Minister for National Education on the advice of the National Council for Higher Education and Research. This new body, created by the law of 1968, is charged with assisting the ministry in the co-ordination of university activities.

Before describing the composition and the role of the National Council for Higher Education and Research, one must underline the need for co-ordination which grew out of the liberation of the universities. At the end of the tumult of 1968 the French government did not go to the lengths suggested by some but only partially adopted the type of system which exists in the United States. It did not want to got so far as to allow total freedom either in the recruitment of students and teachers or in the establishment of operating budgets, fearing that such freedom would give birth to excessive competition between institutions, resulting eventually in marked differences in the value of the degrees granted. The government judged that French customs and attitudes were not ripe to accept such a system.

The system which has developed and which is based on the principles of autonomy and democratic government within the framework of state financing has infused new spirit into the university community. It is now the job of the Ministry of National Education and of its related bodies to assure that the initiatives of the universities are taken in the best interests of all concerned.

Some measures must be adopted to assure harmonious development. First, co-ordination of the decisions taken by various bodies concerned with university affairs is necessary, so as to give their policies some consistency. Second, the definition of curricula and degrees must be carried out.

National Council

The co-ordination of policy rests in the hands of a new council created by the law of 1968, the National Council for Higher Education and Research, mentioned above. It is the last stage in a reconstruction process which started at the base with the creation of the Teaching and Research Units.

The activities of this council are indispensable in the life of the new universities since it must advice the Minister of National Education, who is its president, in the following five areas: planning of teaching and research: establishment of university budgets; definition of national degrees; harmonization between the universities; and judgment in the event of conflict between the rectors and the universities.

The way in which this council will operate is not yet clearly defined. It depends on interrelated problems such as the size of the National Council itself, its composition, and the role which its president, the minister, will wish to play.

The "Orientation" Law of 1968 indicated the percentage of representatives to be taken from each group of electors: full professors, other members of the teaching staff, students, research fellows, administrative personnel, and private individuals. Either a university or a specific discipline is prevented from representation in the National Council unless it has it least 600 participants. On the other hand, to insure the efficiency of the National Council, its size was limited to 90 members. Such a body which has only 32 members of the teaching profession in its ranks cannot represent all the universities, scientific institutions and academic disciplines. If we add the student and administrative members to the teaching members, the total to 54 is still insufficient to represent all the universities. It is for this reason that the minister followed the English and German examples and created a Conference of University Presidents so that every university can make its voice heard at the ministerial level.

The Conference meets real needs. It is normal that the heads of universities should meet periodically to exchange views and to examine questions of mutual interest to their universities. By is official creation the government simply preempted what would naturally have followed. One one hand, the Conference can present its projects and desires to the minister, while on the other, the minister can ask it views when he needs them.

Before a further discussion of the respective roles of the National Council for Higher Education and Research and the Conference of University Presidents, it is important to consider two facts.

The first is that the law of 1968 created only the National Council and made no mention whatsoever of the Conference. The National Council is thus legally preeminent.

The second is that the law of 1968 makes it clear that the National Council gives advice to the minister. The law thus envisaged the National Council, not as a deliberative body, but as an advisory council contributing to the formation of government policies. Under these circumstances the minister wold not be any more constrained by the opinions of his consultative committees than he was before 1968.

The question that can now be asked is how, in fact, each of the three partners conceives his role.

One concepts is that the two consultative bodies are like parliamentary houses between which the minister may act to resolve conflicts. This opinion finds its justification in the fact that the two elective bodies have different bases of support. Since the principle of representation for each university is abandoned, the National Council will be elected from lists proposed at the national level. It will inevitably be the teachers' unions and the students' unions which will draw up those lists.

In such an eventuality, it could be feared that the deliberations of the National Council would be marred by political or social opinions or interdisciplinary quarrels rather than be influenced by enlightened analysis.

On the other hand, the deliberative and advisory roles could be partially assumed by the Conference of Presidents. But here it could be feared that the presidents of the universities, concerned about the budgets for their own institutions and the scarcity of available resources, might not be prepared to map out the guidelines of the new universities which the nation needs.

The bicameral view of the university system does not, however, correspond to reality. Though conflicts of doctrine between the two organs are now impossible, they will not occur frequently. The two bodies will not be called upon to discuss the same topics, and in the event of the matters under consideration being similar, they will be invited to present complementary opinions and view-points.

The National Council and especially its permanent section will be expected to meet frequently in order to carry out the almost daily task of looking at university problems on the national level. It will concern itself with defining the general criteria for allocation of the university budget with the creation of new branches of study and with the validation of degrees. The Conference of University Presidents will be concerned for its part with problems of administration felt at the university level, such as internal organization, campus police, and budgetary administration. It is closer to the truth to say that the presidents of the 67 universities will inform the minister in a realistic way more on the execution of decisions than on doctrinal conceptions likely to orient higher education.

The role of the Minister for National Education will not be diminished by the institutional changes brought about in 1968. He will not so much decide exclusively on points dividing the two representative bodies as be the true center of final decision. It will be his job to allocate the budget. Today the minister deals with 67 universities rather than with the great names of the five faculties of the Universities of Paris, who in the past spoke for their whole field.

The minister thus becomes sort of a catalyst for co-ordination between the universities. More than ever before, he will have to be surrounded by good advisers able to promote higher education while taking into account the views held by all the partners.

Now, these notions must evolve as regards the objectives of higher education, the degrees, and the options available. These necessities will constitute one of the main fields of action of a co-ordination policy; indeed, it can be assumed that the distribution of public financing will be influenced to some degree by the extent to which the decisions reached by the minister, on the advice of the two bodies, are followed.

Degree Structure

The universities of today are largely a regrouping or fragmentation of the old faculties. So far, they have mainly worried about the establishment of their own working rules. During this initial period, without the advice of private, non-academic citizens, objectives were defined in general terms. The degrees to be offered was a main preoccupation, and the question was solved by recourse to the old system: "licence" and "maitrise" in arts, science and social sciences.

The new law provided several possibilities for change in this area. Thus it distinguishes between degrees of a national level, officially recognized throughout France, and degrees of individual universities, which are less homogeneous in quality and object. One of the first areas of co-ordination will be in the establishment of a list of national degrees which will have the advantage of universal recognition. The holders of university degrees, on the other hand, will have to fight themselves to establish the value of their degrees in the market place.

Each national degree will be defined by a few general rules and have a curriculum less explicitly defined than in the past. But it can be feared that the Council's deliberations will only serve to constrain the field of study undertaken so as to be assured of receiving national degree recognition.

During a time of general concern for job security, most teachers and students are criticizing the risks involved with the university degrees as regards subsequent employment. Consequently, it is very likely that the university, will make every effort to obtain the right to offer national degrees. Such an attitude would only serve to raise the value of the national degree at the expense of the university degree. Let it be said that in a more open and dynamic system, the university degree could have served to sanction specialized studies and would undoubtedly have led to stronger innovations.

The concept of a national degree as offering greater security seems to have put the university degree under a cloud. The national degree unites the idea of entrance to a controlled profession with the very different concept of assured employment. It is clear that the experiment of university degree should be carried out at first in a limited number of institutions. If the national degrees appear to constraining and if the university degrees appear too risky, we can have legitimate fear for the progress of higher education.

Thus, the concept of the national must change. The minister has recently shows his concern and has proposed a distinction within the national degree itself between two types of degrees. The first would be a professional degree required for entrance into certain professions like medicine, pharmacy and architecture where the state has to guarantee certain precise qualifications. These degrees would be strictly controlled. The second type of degree would be universally recognized, but the curriculum would be less rigourously centralized. The state would only guarantee the level of studies, whereas their content could be left to the individual universities. An example would be in management science degrees.

The degrees are the end result of different educational streams. The streams themselves are going to require a certain amount of co-ordination. It can be hoped that the National Council and the universities will start realizing the importance of this fact. The universities must establish new streams or options; the job of the National Council and minister will be to circulate information on available curricula and to aid in their selection.

The University and Society

In France the great debate on the relationship between society and the university is still in progress. In co-ordinating their activities, the universities do not avoid the necessity of defining their doctrines in this regard. The range of possible views on the subject is wide: one can discern at one extreme those who wish for a professional university whose sole object would be to turn out a "product" trained according to the demands of employers; at the other, those who wish for a critical university preoccupied only with consent revolution. Most likely the institutions will turn one way or the other or at least state a definite position regarding these problems. These attitudes not being by nature harmonious, the task of the coordinators will be to accept diversity in the experiments, undertaken while bringing information as regards the ultimate aims of the university.

So the National Council for Higher Education and Research and the minister will have to find a just equilibrium between respect for the personality of each university and an enlightened conception of progress in the training of individuals. This task is now being carried out by groups of university teachers and representatives of various professions—industry, agriculture, commerce, finance law and education. These groups have been asked to list the types of higher education needed in each of their branches and to determine their manpower needs in 5 to 15 years' time. They have also been asked to provide a criticism of the present education offered for their profession and to suggest changes which could make it more useful to the student body and to society.

Such work had hardly been undertaken on such a scale until now. It will undoubtedly be a great awakening for the world of the university and will have considerable influence on the determination of new streams of education and options as well as on new teaching methods and degrees. This information will also help improve advanced training and indicate the best ways to keep a balance between early higher education and further periods of training.

Among the major problems which demand co-ordination is the specialization of certain universities in certain regions; the scarcity of financial and human resources and the necessity of creating efficient and optimal teaching and research teams involves certain choices. In our opinion, university co-ordination will be good only insofar as students and teachers can move more easily from one region to another. Not all subjects can be taught at a higher level in all 23 academies and in all 67 universities. Certain choices will have to bee made to prevent the waste of money and human talent.

In conclusion, higher education in France is much more lively with greater university autonomy and the reduction of the university to a more human size.

To capture their vitality and to achieve real progress, the Minister of National Education will have recourse to the opinion of the National Council, elected by the university for this purpose, and the Conference of Presidents. The quality of their recommendations will be decisive even if the minister maintains his freedom of judgment and decision. The value of their advice will depend partially on the topics chosen by these bodies for consideration.

Two pitfalls will make the tasks of the councils difficult. First, it would be unfortunate if the eternal quarrel over budgets were to transform the discussion into bargaining sessions. Second, the diversity in the origins of the members of the councils threatens to introduce political considerations into their recommendations.

Co-ordination of the universities is inevitably a political theme. The French universities must opt for enlightened policies guided by concern for the interests of future generations. Thus can the university become a centre for thought on the future of the individuals it has to train.

Systems of education anywhere and everywhere have to do with people and with persons, with society and with the individual, with a nation and with each citizen. The two aspects belong together. The system reflects the society's history and its present aspirations and goals. This means that systems of higher education in the Caribbean are best understood when they are placed in the context of Caribbean society. It would be more accurate to say "Caribbean societies" since the term "Caribbean" is a geographic one. It does not describe a society or a country. Rather, it refers to a region that is politically the most fragmented, and culturally and ethnically the most diverse in the Americas. The region is a large one, including the archipelago and the mainland countries that border the Caribbean Sea—Venezuela, Colombia—and all the countries of Central America with the exception of EI Salvador.

This statement is concerned with the islands. Their geography and their hostiry explain why as yet there is no such person as a man of the Caribbean; why there is no such thing as a Caribbean society; and why there are in the islands many diverse systems of higher education. Geography and history explain also why there are certain fundamental similarities underlying the dissimilarities, and why efforts as establishing contact between the various systems of higher education are important; indeed are essential.

Cultural Diversity and Similarity

To begin with, the separateness and the separatism. An island is a natural geographic unit, whereas a frontier is arbitrary; but where there are groups of islands, where an archipelago has a geographic focus from which, centripetal forces might operate, it is easier to establish co-operative or regional relationships. The Caribbean archipelago is not a group of islands but a line of islands; and the line is a long time one, extending for 2,000 miles from Cuba to Trinidad. If the islands were drawn together to form one country, it would have an area of 87,000 square miles, the same as Guatemala and Honduras, or about one-fourth the size of Venezuela or one-fifth the size of Colombia. To the separatism born of geography were added antagonisms and rivalries engendered by history. We can form a picture of the political fragmentation that resulted from European colonization by taking the two republics of Guatemala and Honduras, splitting them into 51 parts ranging in size from Cuba's 44,000 square miles to Becquia's 7 square miles, then separating the parts into 6 independent nations, others that are members of the

Kingdom of the Netherlands, others that area part of France, a few British and United States colonies, and one Commonwealth in special relationship with the United States. Following on this, we should people the 51 islands in the way that history did, after removing all the indigenous Indians, for they were destroyed. First, then, the Spaniards, and after them every possible type of European adventurer and settler—Dutch and Portuguese, Jews, prisoners of war and bondservants from England, Scotland and Ireland, militant English Puritans, French Huguenots, Dutch Calvinists, French refugees from the French revolution, Spanish Conservatives seeking refuge from the national liberation movements in Spain. Add hundreds of thousands of Africans moving in year after year for four and a half centuries, making the Caribbean, like North Eastern Brazil and the Deep South of the United States, part of the frontier of Africa. Add also East Indians, who were brought in as estate workers by the thousands over a period of 80 years. To all these add some Chinese, Syrians, Lebanese. The cultural and ethnic diversity is drawn in the landscape, with Spanish-style architecture in Havana, Santo Domingo and San Juan, steep gabled Dutch houses along the waterfront of Curacao, English-style country houses in Barbados, French boulevards in Fort de France. American-style buildings in new San Juan. The impression of cultural diversity is deepened on hearing black men in Curacao speaking Dutch, black men in Martinique speaking French, black men in Jamaica speaking English.

Notwithstanding all this, there are fundamental similarities. Most of the islands have the same physical configuration of a central mountain spine and sculptured valleys. They grow the same slave crops and have the same vegetation. The same historical forces of the and sugar plantation, colonial rule and miscegenation moulded the social configuration of each island. They created a Creole culture which is identifiable as Caribbean.

In these circumstances it seems best to use the case-study method, describing two or three systems of higher education in the Caribbean in greater detail than others, to indicate how, in different ways, the nations of the Caribbean are changing their systems of higher education to meet national needs. Although the focus is on systems of higher education, it is understood that these cannot be set apart from primary and postprimary education. The basic concept is not that of systems arranged neatly in layers. This concept may be logical and tidy, but it is also static and dead. The concept is rather one in which the various systems of education flow into each other, functioning like the circulatory system of the body, interdependent, dynamic, alive.

Higher Education in the Commonwealth Caribbean

The first case study is that of the system of higher education in countries once called the British West Indies and now known as the Commonwealth Caribbean. The University of Guyana is also considered, because Guyana, though on the mainland, is by its history a part of the Commonwealth Caribbean. This case study throws light on the way in which political independence changes a nation's philosophy of education, on the process by which an institution for higher learning patterned on the metro-politan model seeks to adapt and change to meet new needs and goals; on the methods by which a number of small countries with limited resources can establish the maintain a university; on organizational arrangements that enable a university to serve a constituency in separate countries spread out cross 2,000 miles of sea; on the nation-building and personality-building role of universities in developing countries that are predominantly non-European and have a long colonial tradition and an established but often unstated code of white superiority.

Education became a priority with the beginning of a West Indian national movement in the 1930s. The national movement sparked a drive for economic development, and the drive for economic development sparked a drive for education. The whole process was a search for security, a search carried out against a deadline because the newly enfranchised electorate were reaching out for a better way of life after a long period of apathy. Education became the "now thing" not only in the minds of politicians but also in the minds of parents and students. A recent study of Jamaican adolescents shows that both they and their teachers treasured education more than anything else. "Eighty percent of the sample stated that education was the most important "thing" to them......They needed education "in order to get a good job' or 'to amount to somebody in life'...."

The findings of the Jamaica sample are more than substantiated by a study in depth of the aspirations of "Youth in a Developing Society." The country was Trinidad where Blacks and East Indians make up the majority of the island's population. The study revealed the extremely high goals of students with regard to university education. It says that "The highest aspirations in fact are found among the groups formerly least privileged... The pervasive theme among lower middle class students was "We wish to be looked upon." One of the striking "universals" in the study was the expectation of high levels of material consumption, but there was also a forceful theme of social commitment: "Our nation" will need new people to fill the jobs "vacated by the English." This sense of commitment was strongest in those from the lower class. The fact is that in all the former West Indian colonies the social class and ethnic divisions of the society were reinforced by the colonial educational system which developed as a structural consequence of the social system. Independence requires the establishment of a system of education, and especially off higher education, which uses mobility as a new social dynamic. In the words of the report, "High motivation to achievement and to the accompanying emoluments of the consumer culture provide an integrating mechanism in the society. Furthermore, the social commitment of youth can be channelled to the national purpose." This means that opportunity is a crucial factor in the society. The Prime Minister of Trinidad and Tobago emphasized this in his statement that "the real problem is to transfer a satellite economy, satellite of a metropolitan country, with a colonial mentality, into the economy of an independent country that doesn't have a lot of room to manoeuvre."

Three principles governed the expansion of the system of education: that every child should have the opportunity for primary and some form of secondary education; that a centre of higher education should be established; and that the content of education should be changed and made relevant to West Indian circumstances and West Indian needs. It is possible to trace the effects on the University of the West Indies of these radical political and social changes.

The University of the West Indies and the University of Guyana are the only centres of higher education in the Commonwealth Caribbean. The older institution, the University of the West Indies, was founded in 1947 as a co-operative effort by 14 West Indian governments and Britain. It began on the traditional British pattern of a higher-quality small residential college, the target number for enrollment at the end of the first five years being 500. It stressed the importance of high academic work and especially of research. By 1960, it became clear that the earlier principles had to be changed. A policy of expansion was adopted. In

1960 a campus was established in Trinidad, and another in Barbados in 1963. The insistence on residence was abandoned. Night programs was started for part-time students. Enrollment jumped from 900 in 1960 to 5,000 in 1970. The special relationship with the University of London, by which students worked for London degrees, came to an end, and in 1962 the University was given the power to grant its own degrees. New programs were started, such as those in administration, management studies and social work. The University was learning that in a developing country in the contemporary world it had not only to keep its academic standards high but also to study West Indian needs and to help West Indian society to achieve its goals. It continued to insist on high-quality research, because every country, or group of countries, needs at least one centre of excellence where the man of the region can measure himself against international standards. This is especially important in the West Indies where achievement is ego-building; for the bitterest result of slavery was self-contempt, and the bitterest result of colonialism was self-distrust. Also, excellence in academic studies depends heavily on excellence in research; research into the natural products of the region, into medical and agricultural problems, into the factors of social change and of economic development, into the effect of the importation of technology from highly developed industrialized countries with high rates of employment into countries with large rural populations and high rates of unemployment. The research not only established excellence but also enabled the university to make its own unique and essential contribution to national progress. The West Indian experience bears out the statement of Raul Deves, a Chilean engineer and educator, that "underdevelopment exists in the mind of man, and while this mind is not changed, educated and transformed, other efforts will be vain." Also, it reinforces the point made by a former rector of Brasilia, that the fundamental need is training university leaders of the highest capacity and that this can be met only if academic bodies adopt a really mature attitude in regard to the two basic loyalties which every university must respect—responsibility toward the international patterns of learning, and duty toward the social problems of the nation. Without a system of higher education the West Indian countries could have developed neither their own philosophy of education nor of development, nor their own expertise in dealing with the problems of their countries.

Some interesting results have come from this combination of academic excellence with innovation in response to national needs and goals. The organization and structure of the university has been affected. Students have to satisfy certain academic requirements. If they fail to do this after two attempts they withdraw or, in some instances, change their courses of study. The majority of members of the faculty are on a full-time basis and are required to do both teaching and research. The various academic disciplines are grouped together in the traditional way—the natural sciences, the social sciences and the arts, medicine, education and the rest—and these "faculties" are so organized that their work is considered by "faculty boards" assisted by consultative committees that include student members. But the powers and responsibilities of these faculties are limited. They have no autonomy of their own, no rigid organizational structure. They report to a Senate which considers the academic growth of the University as a whole and plans for it. The Senate, which deals primarily with academic subjects, is strongly represented on the supreme governing body of the University, the University Council. This has as members representatives from each of the 14 contributing governments, from the Senate, the Guild of Graduates (the alumni) and the student body. The money to meet recurrent costs and capital expenditure is provided by the various governments on an agreed formula. The pattern of financial support is much the same as that of the United Kingdom where a University Grants Committee examines the request and makes the grant. One important difference is that in the United Kingdom one University Grants Committee deals with the requests of all United Kingdom universities, whereas in the West Indies it is the other way around: the University Grants Committee made up of representatives from 14 different governments deals with the budget of one university. The Grants Committee does this with the help of a small Technical Committee made up of top-ranking civil servants. These say whether the estimates of the University, which are for a three-year period, have been prepared with the necessary forethought and in accordance with agreed policy. They report to the University Grants Committee which considers the requests for funds to meet inescapable current commitments and new developments. The Committee decides how much money the University should receive for a three-year period, each member being empowered to commit his government for the amount due from it.

The West Indian experience of its system of higher education shows the difficulty confronting poor countries when they set themselves to develop satisfactory systems of higher education of good quality and also at the same level of expenditure as rich countries. The traditional pattern in Britain includes expensive honours schools. Since many students entering a university are not research types and do not need to be carried to the frontiers of knowledge, one suggestion is that what they need is a broad education, and for this the United States model of a liberal arts degree may be the more appropriate and the less expensive. Provision can be made for the transfer of the exceptionally gifted student to the major university. It is also becoming clear that the countries of the West Indies cannot afford a large number of highly trained and highly paid specialists in the professions, but that they have to try to provide trained people at three levels: specialists, professionals and sub-professionals. Sir Arthur Lewis, in an article on education and economic development, points out that universities in poor countries have two courses open to them; that of lowering the standards of professional training, which means concentrating on the second level, on the grounds that it is better to have say 100 three-quarter-trained doctors who can be spread over the countryside, rather than 70 well-trained doctors, leaving 30 percent of the population without a doctor. He says, "The alternative policy is to mass produce not the second later but the third and in the process even to upgrade the training of the third level. One then floods the countryside not with low grade dentists but with high grade dental assistants. If this policy is adopted the corollary is to upgrade the training not only of the third layer but also for the second layer. For the second layer professional now has many more third layer people working under him.... From this it follows that he needs an even sounder training than his professional colleague in Europe...."

There is an interesting between the systems of higher education in Guayana and the other English-speaking countries of the Caribbean. Guyana joined with the other West Indian governments in setting up the University of the West Indies in 1947, but in the 1960s, she decided to set up her own university. After doing this she made an agreement with the University of the West Indies by which a specified number of Guyanese are admitted each year to the professional schools of the University of the West Indies.

The arrangements by which the two systems of higher education buttress each other in the training of professional people points to one of the ways in which Caribbean countries might find a solution to the almost intractable problem of rising costs. Developed countries, confronted with the same problem, are finding a solution in the grouping of universities, but what are small countries to do? Or developing countries whose future depends on the utilization of their resources, but who have to spend more than they have on education in order to do this? Certainly the developing countries need to study the solutions being tried by richer countries, but it may well be that they should give as much attention to experiments and solutions being tried by countries in the same position as themselves.

In this connection three programs of work in the University of the West Indies may be of interest. One is for teachers in the field, both primary and post-primary. A Department of Education in the University undertakes the professional training of the teacher, but the outward reaching arm of the university for the in-service training of teachers in the field is a specially created Institute of Education. The members of the staff of this institute are dispersed at centres in the Caribbean, and in many respects they do the work of extension officers in teacher training. Similarly, the adult education program of the university is in the hands of full-time university staff employed on the same terms as all other faculty, based on university centres, one in each supporting country. The third outward-reaching arm is an Institute of Social and Economic Research. Its primary functions are to do research and to serve as advisers or consultants to supporting governments. One of the difficulties that the university faced in its early years was that there was no corpus of knowledge in economics or sociology or administration that was relevant to the Caribbean. Through its research the Institute of Social and Economic Research has done much to correct this.

Higher Education in Surinam and the Netherlands Antilles

Before turning to the systems of higher education in Puerto Rico and in the Dominican Republic, reference should be made to the position of higher education in the Netherlands Antilles and Surinam and in the Caribbean Departments of France. Each of these two groups, like Puerto Rico and the West Indies, has been concerned with securing economic viability and autonomy. Can a small country with limited resources have both? Why should independence or autonomy be for the large and rich and for the large and poor but not for the small and poor? What per capita income should a country have before it establishes its own system of higher education? Or what proportion of its children should be in secondary schools? How many trained people can it absorb? The Dutch countries attempted to find economic viability and yet attain autonomy when, in 1954, they set up a Kingdom of the Netherlands consisting of three states: Surinam, the six small islands grouped together as the Netherland Antilles and Holland. Each state has its own constitution, and Surinam and the Antilles have a great measure of autonomy in local affairs. The ties between the Antilles and Holland go back to the 1930s, and the educational system is closely modelled on that of Holland Schooling is thorough, and there is an efficient teacher training college in Curacao, but the total population is only about a quarter million, and there is no university, though there are plans for a law school. Surinam has a small law school which is being expanded, and it is setting up a medical school with a great deal of assistance from the University of Leyden. The fact that there is no joint effort by Surinam and the Antilles indicates how deep rooted is Caribbean separatism, even between countries speaking the same language.

The French colonies of Guiana, Martinique and Guadeloupe chose to follow a very different course. Determined not to remain colonies, and at the same time seeking economic security, they chose to be assimilated into France as Departments. As far as higher education is concerned, the high school student in Martinique and

Guadeloupe looks forward to becoming a university student in France, at the University of Paris, the University of Bordeaux and others. At present, the University of Bordeaux has in hand the development of a School of Medicine in Martinique and of a School of Agronomy in Guadeloupe, but certainly for some time to come the system of higher education will be that of France.

Higher Education in Puerto Rico

The second case study for consideration is that of higher education in Puerto Rico, an island which presents the usual Caribbean contrast of a physical family likeness alongside cultural dissimilarities. For example, Puerto Rico and Jamaica share many physical features, but they are very different in population and social development. During the period that Jamaica became a sugar- and slave-plantation island, Puerto Rico, a Spanish military outpost in the Caribbean, was an island of free smallholders, mostly of European origin. After the 1830s when slavery was brought to an end in Jamaica and the large estates fell into ruin, Jamaica became a country of landed peasants, predominantly black, for the number of slaves had been as high as 90 percent of the island's population. At that very time Puerto Rico was becoming a sugar plantation islands, and the sugar estates were eating up the smallholdings. Sugar squeezed the Puerto Rican smallholder off his holding and transformed him into a landless estate worker. Slaves were employed also, but the percentage of slaves in the population never rose above 10 percent.

Contrasts and differences notwithstanding, Puerto Rico shared the experience of the English-speaking sugar islands, for after a period of prosperity there came a slump and hard times. Like Jamaica and sister islands, she also had a long period of colonial rule, 400 years of it under Spain, then in 1898 a transfer to the United states. Like Jamaica and

Martinique and Curacao she also had to find economic viability and at the same time autonomy. Luis Munoz Marin and his Popular Party, campaigning under the emblem of the peasant's hat, the "pavo", swept to power in the 1940s and provided an answer, that of a Commonwealth in free association with the United States. The political and economic transformation that has taken place in the last quarter of a century is well known, but one aspect should be emphasized here—the impressive contribution made by Puerto Rican intellectuals. In a comprehensive study of Puerto Rico, Gordon Lewis makes a statement that is valid for the systems of higher education in the West Indies as well as in Puerto Rico, that the educational process becomes much more than an intellectual experience or the privilege of elite groups. It is a vehicle of social mobility, "a mechanism whereby new graduating classes learn not only to understand society but also to manipulate it." In the colonial period the intellectual led the nationalist movement. "The second generation of protest" sought a more fundamental reorganization of the social and economic structure of society. The record shows that the Puerto Rican system of higher education provided a number of eminently qualified Puerto Ricans ready to lead their country in the 1940s, at a time of radical social and political change.

The figures indicate that very nearly two out of every 100 Puerto Ricans are in institutions of higher education. This is about twice the level in most Western European countries and very nearly half of that in the United States. To reach a comparable level the University of the West Indies would need to have an enrollment of 60,000, about 12 times the present number. But there is a financial aspect to all this. A recent report concerning higher education facilities in Puerto Rico examined the specifications laid down by the United States Office of Education for university plants and equipment and stated that an estimated $259,380,000 would be required by Puerto Rico. It went on to say that "only if a massive Federal grant and loan program were instituted in this year... would it be possible to achieve the standards laid down by the United States Office of Education." No possibilities of financing on this scale are available to the University of the West Indies or the University of Guyana.

The Puerto Rican experience illustrates the nation-building role of a system of higher education. Because the system was established about 70 years ago, because in 1942 legislation opened the way for university reforms, and because it was a major objective of the University to make an impact on the whole society, the University of Puerto Rico became a nursery for local and administrative leadership. The Puerto Rican system of higher education also promoted social mobility in much the same way as the West Indian system of higher education. We have already noted the effect on the youth of Trinidad. There is a further point to be made: that both the West Indian system of higher education and the larger more complex Puerto Rican system are committed to the overall planning of higher education. In 1964 an Executive Order by the Governor of Puerto Rice created a Commission for the Advancement of Higher Education, and in 1967 this commission arranged for a study of the space needs of institutions of higher education in the island, with a projection of enrollments and of faculty increase, bearing in mind the needs of various regions of the island, population distribution and the like. The planning was to be done by the University of Puerto Rico but—and this is important—in consortium with order accredited institutions of higher education. The report recommended the sharing of existing and projected facilities in order to facilitate closer co-operation among the various institutions of higher education.

The Dominican Republic, Haiti, and Cuba

Half a jet hour away to the west of San Juan is one of

the oldest universities in the Americas, the University of Santo Domingo. If forms an important part of the system of higher education of the Dominican Republic. There are two private universities, the University of Madrey Maestra at Santiago and the University of Pedro Henriquez Urena in Santo Domingo. Whereas in Puerto Rico there are no basic differences between the private and public universities, there are marked differences between the private universities in the Dominican Republic and the University of Santo Domingo, which was founded in the Spanish tradition and which was made autonomous in 1962. It includes faculties of law, medicine, economics, engineering, philosophy and a school of agriculture and animal husbandry. The student body is politically active. The two private universities are more closely related in their organization structure to the Puerto Rican universities and to a number of the new universities in Latin America. Consequently, though there are possibilities for inter-institutional co-operation, it is more difficult to achieve this in the Dominican Republic than it is in Puerto Rico or the Commonwealth Caribbean. The two private universities were founded in the early 1960s and they are developing impressive new campuses with modern facilities.

Haiti shares the island of Hispaniola with the Dominican Republic, having a third of the land area and about 750,000 more people. The population density is 400 persons to the square mile. Many of the square miles are eroded, and many of the persons illiterate, possibly 85 out of every 100. Eighty-seven out of 100 live in rural areas, a higher proportion than in any country in Latin America. The per capita income is of the order of $70 (U.S.) The figures indicate the desperate shortage of education in the country. When Haiti became independent in 1803 there were no schools. It was then the colony of St. Domingue, the boast of France as a sugar-producing colony; and as in Jamaica at that time the only training for the mass of the population was through the "pickney gang," the gang of children who, under the direction of an elderly black slave, were driven to weeding and gathering fodder for livestock. A century and a half later the country had some 3,500 schools, public and private. In Port Prince there are excellent bookshops with the latest French writing. There is an appreciation of scholarship and a literary tradition. Haitian intellectuals like Price Mars were among the first in the Caribbean to turn the eyes of the black man toward his own rich heritage, his folklore, his authentic belongings. But such education as existed was modelled on that of France. It remained the monopoly of an elite. The curriculum was literary rather than relevant. Leyburn, in his perceptive and sympathetic work, *The Haitian People*, said that teachers trained in this tradition might teach Racine and Montaigne but not soil conservation and new methods of planting. The contrast with the Second Until Schools of Puerto Rico and the Vocational Training Centres of Jamaica could not be more striking, more harsh. The fact is that the Haitian peasant world is not the world of the Haitian educated. Its language is Creole, whereas classes are in French, and as Leyburn points out, Creole is as different from French as Dutch from German. Haiti has tried to correct the weakness in education. In the decade of the 1950s the number of pupils in primary schools increased by 15 percent. Yet in 1960, only one-fourth out of the 990,000 children of primary school age in Haiti attended school. As far as higher education is concerned, the two important subjects are law and medicine, the traditional ones which lead to status and security.

Haiti lies next door to Cuba, the largest island in the archipelago, as large as all the other islands put together. Jamaica is only 90 miles to the south. Yet the distance cannot be measured in geographic terms. The attitude in many of the islands was that Castro's revolution had removed Cuba from the Caribbean. In recent years, however, educators and others have begun to see that the island still forms part of the archipelago and that events in Cuba are a part of Caribbean history.

It appears as if, during the first phase of the Cuban revolution, the government's chief concern was to redistribute income. It was during this period, in 1959 and 1962 that agrarian reforms were carried through expropriating holdings of large landowners, nationalizing large estates, and redistributing the land to the peasants. During this period the government aimed at moving from an agricultural economy into an industrialized one. In the second phase national effort centred on production. The government, using education as a tool of national development and as a means of integrating Cuba's peasant population into the new Cuban society, set about the task of making the peasant literate, and of improving scientific and technological studies. A new system of education was created for the express purpose of meeting the national goals of an integrated, productive society. In 1961 an attack was launched on illiteracy. The peasant had been isolated in rural areas by bad roads and by poor schooling. Of every 109 peasants, 43 were illiterate. In country areas 60 out of every 100 children of school age did not attend school. Out of the total number of children that reached the sixth form in primary schools, only 20 percent were from the rural area. The per capita income of the peasant was one-third that of the national per capita income. Through a literacy campaign these deficiencies were dramatized. The campaign swept educated youth into the campaign as a task of social reconstruction. A task force of about 300,000 teachers was created that included 100,000 secondary school students and 30,000 teachers. A Unesco report emphasized that not only was the effort well organized but that personal contact contributed greatly to its success.

The figures that are available point to an impressive widening of educational opportunity. In 1969 there were

700,000 children in secondary schools, twice as many as ten years earlier. Over the same period the number in intermediary education increased three-fold. According to the Cuban Ministry of Education the number of students in institutions of higher education rose to 29,000 in 1969, and the number of professors was 4,300. University enrollment should grow more quickly in the 1970s, because there are now some 80,000 pupils in secondary schools. Before 1959 university education followed the traditional Hispanic pattern with an emphasis on law, medicine and humanistic studies. A recent article in *Science* by a distinguished Latin American scientist, Marcel Roche, quotes figures supplied by the University of Havana which reveal a sharp change in direction. In 1959 just over 37 percent of the students were in the humanities. In 1968-69 the proportion was 6 percent. The proportion in medicine remained much the same, 28 percent and 30 percent. In education the proportion fell from 19 percent to 8 percent. In science the proportion rose from 7 percent to 16 percent, in technology from 5 percent to 26 percent, in agriculture and veterinary science from 3 percent to 7 percent, and in economics from 6 percent to 6 percent. The statistics take on flesh and blood and come to life in an account Roche gives of a conversation with students at a field school, Escuela de Campo, near Havana. About 80 students gathered around him, "most of them 11 to 12 years old, and I asked a number of them what they wanted to be when they grew up. All whom I questioned knew the answer without hesitation: 'mechanical engineer, physicist, chemical engineer,' and in the case of one girl 'military communications.' When I asked specifically how many would take up a career in the humanities, law, history or philosophy, no hands were raised. Although career choice is free it is clear that the policy of the government and the general orientation of the schools have profoundly modified the motivation of students. Incidentally the increase in total university enrollment has been far from spectacular as compared with increases in most Latin American countries."

The growth in university enrollment in science and technology is parallelled by a growth in scientific research in the university and also in specialized university institutions such as CENIC, the National Scientific Research Centre; ICA, the Institute of Animal Science; and the Victoria de Giron Institute which is a centre for basic medical science.

There is some basic research and a good deal of applied research. For example, the Institute of Animal Science is working on such problems in animal nutrition as finding a satisfactory food for cattle which contains a high percentage of diluted molasses as well as other products of the sugar cane. This is so because Cuba is expanding its cattle industry, making the fullest use of all possible products from its sugar industry. Through the research institutes and the system of higher education, research is being directed to solving problems in number of industries. An example is the fishing industry in which national production has trebled since 1959.

The support the Government has given to science and technology and the public image of the scientist and technologist at work on problems of production has strengthened public appreciation, but it remains to be seen to what extent basic research will flourish. The new attitude is described by Roche: He found that the postgraduate students with whom he talked felt they were useful to the community and they knew that the level of support for their work was considerable. He concluded, "Life is austere for the Cubans but, at least for the scientists, it is bracing and stimulating."

Conclusion

We have traversed thus far some 3,000 miles, moving

from Surinam and Guyana on the South American mainland through the archipelago, following the route that the indigenous people of the islands, the Arawaks and Caribs, took many centuries before the birth of Christ. We have moved up the arc of islands from Trinidad and Barbados to Hispaniola, once the centre of the Spanish American empire, and to Cuba. We have seen that the history of the region is written deep in the systems of higher education, and we have found abundant evidence of a new dynamism generated within the countries of the region by political change and economic pressures. Today 150,000 university students crowd the colleges and institutions of the region, and pressing on their heels there is a vast crowd of pupils in secondary schools. Their father were desperately concerned with dependence and economic development. Today's generation appears less moved by economic than by social and by broad political issues: by the need for changing the traditional Caribbeal attitudes of dependence and rivalry; by a rejection of external economic domination, by a rejection of any form of racial discrimination. Blackness had become a dominant theme. And like students everywhere today, the Caribbean student organizations are in a hurry. The last words of the study of the aspirations of youth in Trinidad bear on the point that "The development of the society will tell the story of the students chances and achievements. One thing is certain; having looked upward to the future, they will never be content with a return to the past." This sense of commitment is stronger when the student studies in a local university. Recently Jamaica was used as a case study for the emigration of high-level manpower and national development, and one of the conclusions was that the group of Jamaican university graduates that emigrates is mostly composed of graduates of overseas universities. The finding is that many overse as graduates do not return to Jamaica to reside after graduation; and that though graduates from the University of the West Indies emigrate, the proportion is much lower.

Today the jet liner and telecommunications, atomic energy and satellites have so reduced our world that the continents have shrunk to the size of islands. They have taken away the buffer of distance that once kept men of different races and cultures apart from each other. The problems of the space age spring from speed and proximity; and the educator of the space age is faced with the problem of using technology and at the same time deepening understanding not only of a country and a people but of the wold and of all people. There is no escape from this. In the words of Adlai Stevenson, all men are now travellers on a space ship from which there is no escape hatch. In these circumstances the diversity and variety that characterize the Caribbean become advantages. They offer countless opportunities for contact with, and understanding of, people of many diverse groups and cultures. Seeking to use these opportunities, the universities and research centres of the region, including not only the islands but also some universities in Venezuela, Colombia, Mexico, Louisiana, and Florida, have founded an Association of Caribbean Universities and research Institutes for the purpose of working together in areas critical to Caribbean development, such as health, food, teacher education, population studies, science and technology. Already they are exploring ways of using technology to spread specialist resources, of sharing library resources, and of working together in research projects. Taken together; the members of the Association constitute a powerful regional resource of scholarship and of experience gained in the Caribbean. This attempt, however modest, represents a rejection of the old separateness and separatism. Whatever happens, we know now that the old ideas will not do.

4

California Education in America

Public higher education in California is barely more than one century old. It began officially in 1968 when the State Legislature passed a law creating the University of California. From that time the public system has grown from a single, tiny campus in Berkeley to a massive and diversified complex. The handful of students in the pioneer freshman class of the university in 1869 has increased to an enrollment of more than a million students in public institutions of higher education. The number of separate campuses has grown from one in the beginning to more than 120. Its annual budget of a few thousand dollars a year in 1868 grew to a total of one and one-half billion dollars in 1968. In terms of sheer magnitude of growth it would be difficult to find a comparable century in the entire history of education.

As the system has grown, moreover, three distinct tiers, or segments, have emerged. The university was guaranteed constitutional status with a Board of regents as its governing body from its beginning. For the first half-century Berkeley dominated the system as the only general campus, though special professional schools were established in San Francisco. Political pressure from southern California led to the opening of a southern branch with university status, which officially became the University of California at Los Angeles (UCLA) in 1927. Subsequently a number of specialized research stationns—for example, at Davis and Riverside—were converted into general campuses, and in the 1960s several new campuses were opened. At present the University of California is truly a "multiversity", with nine campuses, and a total enrollment in excess of 100,000 students.

University

Though its functions have changed from time to time, the university has always maintained its place at the apex of the system of higher education from the standpoint of research, professional training, and granting of degrees. The education code of the state declares that the university is "the primary state-supported academic agency for research;" that it has "exclusive jurisdiction in public higher education, in the professions of law, and over graduate instruction in the professions of medicine, dentistry, veterinary medicine and architecture;" and that it "has the sole authority in public higher education to award the doctoral degree in all fields of learning."

State Colleges

The California State Colleges, the second segment, had their unofficial beginnings even earlier than the university, with the establishment of the San Jose State Normal School as a teacher training institution in 1862. Seven more normal schools were established by 1919; the legislature authorized the normal schools to become teachers' colleges in 1921, and to confer the bachelor's degree in 1923. By 1935 the word "teachers" was dropped and these institutions became general state colleges. Legislation in 1949 permitted them to grant the master's degree in education, and in the middle 1950s they began offering masters' degrees in selected non-teaching fields. The legislation establishing the Master Plan for Higher Education, in 1960, permitted state colleges to grant doctoral degrees jointly with the university. Finally, the education code authorizes faculty research in the state colleges "to the extent that it is consistent with the primary function of the state colleges and the facilities provided for that function."

The history of the state colleges, then, has been one of the continuous expansion and upgrading of functions. As we shall see, this process has been accompanied by intense competition between the state colleges and the university—competition which is far from resolved at the present time. Quantitatively, the colleges grew at a very modest rate in the early decades, reaching a total of only 13,000 students by 1940. Growth in the postwar years was phenomenal, however, with the system moving from an enrollment of 33,500 in 1950 at almost 225,000 in 1969.

Junior Colleges

The third public sector, the California Junior Colleges—or community colleges, as they are now often called—had its official beginning in 1907, when the Legislature authorized legislation enabling high school and other districts to offer instruction beyond the high school level. In 1910 the first public junior college was established in Fresno. While not the first state to introduce public junior colleges, California was the most prolific in developing them. By 1950 total enrollment in junior colleges was 134.585, and, like the state colleges, they attained an extraordinary rate of growth in the 1950s and 1960s, reaching an enrollment of more than 700,000 by 1969. The state supports more than 90 public college campuses in all.

Though some two-years junior colleges have been converted into four-years institutions, the norm has been that junior colleges offer course work for only two years after graduation from high school. In 1960, when the junior colleges were incorporated into the system of higher education by the Master Plan legislation, they were expressly limited to two-years status and to awarding the associate in arts and associate in science degrees. The legislation further specified that instruction should be primarily in three areas: "(1) standard collegiate courses for transfer to higher institutions; (2) vocational and technical fields leading to employment; and (3) general or liberal arts courses."

The general picture of public higher education in California, then, is one of extremely rapid growth within a three-tiered system that has managed, despite-some overlapping, to maintain a fairly strict differentiation of function. Each segment offers instruction in the arts and sciences. The university is the exclusive guardian of research and of training associated with high-prestige occupations (medical, legal, academic etc.); the state colleges prepare students for more advanced academic work and train students for a supplementary range of occupations, especially teaching; the junior colleges prepare students for more advanced academic work and train them for more vocational types of occupations. The differentiation of functions among the segments, therefore, roughly parallels the stratification of the system of occupational roles in the larger society, for which the students of each segment are destined.

Each of the segments, in its own functional sphere, has developed into a kind of national model. The University of California is regarded in many quarters as the greatest public university system in the country; two of its campuses, Berkeley and UCLA, rank among the highest in the nation in graduate training and research. Among state college systems the California State Colleges are perhaps the most highly developed, and the junior colleges have always been at the forefront of the junior colleges movement in the United States. This obvious point must be made, because the system has also been beset by many troubles, and to focus on these troubles—as I shall do later—might obscure the substantial accomplishments of the system. It is my belief, moreover—and I shall amplify this later as well—

that the same social forces that have contributed to its growth and eminence have simultaneously been responsible for some of its troubles.

What are the general factors that have led to such a rapid and continuous growth of the California system of public higher education? Any enumeration of these factors must be approximate and oversimplified, but the following seem to have been the most important:

(1) California, as one of the newer, but larger and more prosperous states in the United States, has always had a fiercely competitive outlook, especially in regard to the older and more "established" states in the East. With respect to higher education, this outlook has manifested itself in the impulse to build a bigger and better system. This competitive outlook, in my opinion, has contributed more than any other single factor to the elitist impulse in California's higher education. This elitism, bred by attitudes of regional competitiveness rather than aristocratic values, has contributed to the continued generosity of California's public to a university of exceptionally high quality.

(2) At the same time, values of populism and equality of opportunity are also deeply rooted in California's culture. Among the most democratic of states in social outlook, California could be expected to give mass support to higher education as it came to be regarded as one of the principal avenues of social mobility. In particular, this outlook contributed to the spread of the junior colleges, which were ultimately to guarantee an opportunity in some kind of institution of higher education for every high school graduate in California. This populist tradition has also fostered an attitude of ambivalence toward the university, which has been regarded simultaneously as a source of state pride and as a focus for the expression of sentiments of anti-intellectualism and political suspicion.

(3) As California developed from one of the most backward regions of the country in the mid-nineteenth century into the most urbanized—and one of the most industrialized—states in the country, its demands for urban and industrial occupations (such as engineering, medicine, nursing, law, social work, city planning, criminology), to say nothing of highly skilled labor, have multiplied correspondingly. It fell mainly to the system of higher education to train people for these new and more demanding occupational roles. To do so, their facilities had to be expanded accordingly.

(4) California moved from a thinly populated region in the mid-nineteenth century to the most populous state in the nation in the late 1960s. While population growth has been impressive throughout California's history, it has been especially pronounced in the period following World War II. Also, the proportion of persons of student age (18-24) was higher in California in that period than in the rest of the country, and the expectation that a person in that age-range would be enrolled in an institution of higher education was higher in California than in the nation as a whole. The demographic pressure on California's system of higher education has therefore been very strong, especially in the past two decades.

(5) California has always been a prosperous state; its opportunities to devote substantial resources to education have been correspondingly greater than those of its less opulent sister states. When the federal government and the private foundations opened their coffers to support higher education in the 1950s and 1960s. California received its share of these funds, and its opportunities for educational expansion were further enlarged.

(6) Besides being competitive with other states and other regions, California is also characterized by a brisk internal competition—between northern and southern California,

between valley and coast, between rural and urban, between one community and another. As educational institutions came to be regarded as a source of local wealth and prestige, communities and regions came to vie for campuses of their own. This political situation in California augmented the impulse for growth of the system; it also fostered fierce competition for resources within each segment of the higher education and among the various segments.

This blending of social and cultural forces—a commitment to the values of excellence and egalitarianism, a pervasive competitive spirit, the pressure of numbers, and the opportunities of affluence—have propelled California's system of higher education in its remarkable century of growth. Let us now turn to some of the problems that have accompanied that process of growth.

The Pains of Growth

One of the general characteristics of rapidly growing social systems is that they are forever threatening to outgrow those very structures that have been designed to regulate their functioning. This has been true to some extent for each segment of California's system of higher education, and certainly true for the system as a whole.

To illustrate: In the early years of the university, the Board of Regents was able to consider each faculty appointment individually, and to attend to very minor financial details. The university was small and uncomplicated. As Berkeley grew and as new campuses began to develop, however, such detailed regulation of day-by-day administration by the Regents and the central administration became progressively more difficult. In a 1955 report, a team designated to restudy the needs of California higher education complained that the Regents' docket was burdened with unnecessary details, and recommended that the business of the Board should be decentralized so that it could give more attention to general matters of educational policy. Some steps were taken in this direction in subsequent years, and in 1965-66, when it was believed by many that too centralized control had contributed in part to the crises of academic authority during the Free Speech Movement in 1964-65, the Board of Regents undertook to accelerate the process of delegating Regental and statewide administrative authority to the several campuses. As a result of this decentralization, "the Board of Regents has become less an administrative board and more a policy board, and the University...has become less a monolithic structure and more pluralistic in character." Nevertheless, the issue of Regental authority is not yet stabilized. Despite the general movement toward decentralization, the Regents have periodically elected to restore previously delegated authority to themselves, particularly in times of crisis and insensitive areas—such as the appointment and promotion of politically controversial faculty members—much to the consternation of chancellors and faculties. It might reasonably be asked whether a board, meeting only once a month for a few days, is till a viable mechanism for governing—even at a general policy level—so large and complex a system as the university has become.

The regulation of the remainder of the system has posed even greater difficulties. Until 1960, the entire public education system except for the university—primary, elementary, and secondary education, including junior colleges and state colleges—was under the administrative direction of the State Board of Education, and the chief executive officer of educational activities was the State Superintendent of Public Instruction. As early as the 1930s, however, it became apparent that public education was much too cumbersome to the regulated by that kind of agency. In 1939 the Curriculum Co-ordinator for the California State Colleges complained that:

> [the system of control by the State Board of Education] has not been without its difficulties. Some overlappings of functions, some confusion as to policy and some barren areas have resulted...These difficulties could not have been foreseen because the... system of educational control was set up before the emergence of present teacher training requirements and standards of certification, before the development of the junior college system and before the ...state colleges came into being.

In the postwar period of growth of the junior colleges and state colleges it became progressively clearer that a single state agency could not be an effective governing device for such a complex system. Two of the reforms associated with the Master Plan and its implementation were the creation of a separate Board of Trustees for the state colleges in 1960, and the creation of a separate Board of Governors for the junior colleges in 1967, thus paring back the jurisdiction of the Board of Education to primary and secondary education.

A general process thus seems to have repeated itself in the history of California higher education: the system—or part of it—is placed under relatively centralized governing machinery at some point in its history; as its growth proceeds apace, however, the system becomes progressively less governable by the original machinery; at a certain point a crisis of governance occurs; and, after a period of turmoil, new, more, decentralized governing structure is invented and institutionalized.

The growth of the system has also been punctuated by episodes of intense competition within the segments and among the segments. Many at Berkeley bitterly opposed the establishment of the Los Angeles campus, and, during the deliberations leading to the Master Plan, several chancellors of the existing university campuses expressed apprehension that the development of several new campuses would occasion a decline in resources available to the established campuses. And under the Master Plan, the university campuses have continued to vie with one another for resources, prestige, and power. Berkeley has struggled to maintain its flaggship status among the campuses, and the Joint Committee on Higher Education of the California Legislature recently remarked that "University campuses such as Santa Cruz and Riverside are. . . locked into the general University mold which, despite some important differences in organization, emphasis and outlook, forces them to rush ahead in the tracks of Berkeley and UCLA," Similar competitive pressures for scarce resources—and a tendency for a more or less equitable response to these pressures on the part of state authorities who control the resources—have also made for a movement toward uniformity and competition-inspired growth within the state college and junior college systems.

Competition among the segments has been much more intense than within the segments. In the 1920s the state teachers' colleges were coming into their own, and the junior college system was developing rapidly; also in that decade California's population increased by almost two-thirds. This combination of population pressure and opportunity to grow gave rise to a brisk "regional college" movement as well as a movement to convert some junior colleges into four-year colleges. This provoked sharp opposition from the university officials, who feared that an unrestricted number of four-years, general-function colleges would be created by the legislature in response to local pressures. The impulse to convert junior colleges into four-year colleges was also felt immediately after World War II.

The most intense period of segmental competition appeared in the mid-1950s. The state was faced with an enormous cohort of school-age children who were about to enter institutions of higher education. Dozens of bills for new colleges, or for changing the functions of existing ones, were introduced into the Legislature on behalf of cager localities between 1955 and 1959. The growth guidelines of the liaison committee of the Board of Regents and the State Board of Education were openly disregarded in the dash for new institutions. Educators in the university, the private sector, and the junior college sector feared that the higher education system would degenerate into a chaotic expansion of state colleges through pork-barrel legislation. And many feared that if the system could not come up with some plan for coordination and rational growth, the legislature, though ill-equipped to co-ordinate the systems, would nevertheless take matters into its own hands. Such were the problems that stimulated the effort to develop some Master Plan to co-ordinate the entire system in the late 1950s.

As we shall see, the Master Plan was directed in part at resolving and regulating these competitive struggles. It has proved successful in part. Nevertheless, the competition between the state colleges and the university has continued to the present. The state colleges have launched a multipronged offensive to achieve university status, attempting to gain research funds and sabbatical privileges for their faculty, and attempting—and almost succeeding—in securing a change of name whereby they would become California State Universities.

Efforts to Co-ordinate

Earlier I noted a kind of periodicity in the growth of

California's higher education, involving the phases of centralization, growth, crises of governance and decentralization. A similar cycle has repeated itself with respect to competition and co-ordination among the segments. The cycle begins with some kind of crisis of competition: this gives rise to some "study commission" of investigation, which attempts to devise a new framework for integration and co-ordination; next at attempt is made to implement the recommendations; and finally competition begins to develop within the new framework.

To illustrate: in the midst of the regional college movement of the early 1930s the Legislature commissioned the Carnegic Foundation for the Advancement of Teaching to conduct a study of the California system of higher education. Among the proposals of this commission was that the Legislature establish a State Council for Educational Planning and Co-ordination. This was established in 1933, but since it was a purely advisory body, it could not enforce any recommendations regarding the growth and coordination of the system. It was largely ineffectual as a co-ordinating device, and ceased its activities by 1941.

In 1945 the Board of Regents and the State Board of Education created, on an informal basis, a Liaison Committee which would issue non-binding proposals regarding plans and projects that might affect the system as a whole. The Liaison Committee achieved some success in stemming the movement toward four-year status on the part of the junior colleges, in reaffirming the principles of differentiation among the several segments, and in dampening the growth of new institutions. A proposal to expand and reorganize the liaison machinery was made in 1955, but by that time action of this sort could not be seriously contemplated, because the state had entered the period of competitive chaos of the late 1950s.

The Master Plan for Higher Education marked one of the most comprehensive co-ordinative efforts in the history of American education. In one sense it represented a great political compromise among the various segments. It provided certain benefit for each. To the junior colleges it afforded a status in the higher education system for the first time, and granted them a major role in realizing the egalitarian goal of a place for every high school graduate in an institution of higher education. To the private sector it also granted a formal place in the planning and co-ordinating machinery for the first time. To the university it afforded protection for its research and degree-granting functions. And to the state colleges it afforded higher admission standards, the joint doctorate, the extension of master's degrees, its own Board of Trustees, and more liberal policies on faculty research. The one advantage the state colleges did not gain was a constitutional status parallel to that of the university. The colleges still remain the creations of legislative statute. Some now maintain that this was a serious failure. Constitutional status, it is argued, would have given the state colleges a legal status parallel to the university, and would have given them greater budgetary independence from the legislature than they now enjoy. Furthermore, it would have given constitutional delineation to their functions, thus discouraging political agitation on their part to change these functions, which would require a new constitutional amendment.

So much for the short-term significance of the Master Plan as a political compromise. In the longer term it provided two sources of co-ordination for the system. First, it reaffirmed the main lines of functional differentiation among the segments. In the work of the Survey Team and anxiliary committees, moreover, it provided long-term estimates and policies for the rates of growth for the several segments with respect to lower-division, upper-division, and graduate students; policies for the transfer of students from sector to sector; admissions policies for the several sectors; a policy for the adoption of year-round operations. Second, and perhaps more important, it provided a Co-ordinating Council for Higher Education, which has provided to be the most important co-ordinating body in the history of the system.

In the planning stages for the Master Plan, all parties recognized the need for more comprehensive and forceful co-ordinating machinery for the system as a whole. Many separate ideas were floated, including the idea of a superboard of governors, which would have had binding regulative authority over all the segments. Because of the unwillingness of each of the segments to sacrifice this much of their autonomy, however, and because of the Legislature's reluctance to renounce this much of its traditional control, the Co-ordinating Council for Higher Education that was finally created in 1960 was much weaker than a superboard. It was originally composed of 15 members, three each from the University Board of Regents, the State College Board of Trustees, the junior colleges, and the private sector of higher education; and three public members appointed by the Governor. Its functions were advisory to each segment and to the Legislature and the Governor, and it had no binding authority. Its assigned activities were to review the budgetary and capital outlay requests of the public segments and to comment on the general level of financial support sought by the system; to play a sort of watchdog role with respect to the principle of functional differentiation, assuring that each sector played its assigned role and attempting to avoid duplication among the sectors; and to plan for the orderly growth of each of the sectors—including the addition of new campuses—within the confines of the general policies set by the Survey Team for the Master Plan.

The Co-ordinating Council has met with only mixed success. It has eliminated barriers to the transfer of students from junior colleges to the other segments; it has avoided a certain amount of duplication among the three segments; it has assumed administrative responsibility for the allocation of considerable sums of federal money to the various segments; it has played an important advisory role in limiting the establishment of new campuses during the past decade; it has made space utilization more rational; and in dozens of staff reports, it has supplied information valuable for short and long-term planning.

Yet on many other counts the Council has failed. Most notable is its failure to have any impact on the budgetary review. Part of this failure rests with the fact that the Council had neither the capacity nor the authority to issue policies that would be guaranteed to influence the Governor, the State Department of Public Finance, the Legislature, or the individual segments. Furthermore, the three segments tended to press their budgetary claims independently of—not through—the Co-ordinating Council. In certain other areas as well the Council was by passed by the segments. Meeting initially with an unfriendly response to their drive for university status, the state colleges turned directly to Legislative influence. Thus the Council has proved ineffective in areas that are of monumental concern to each segment, partly because it lacks the necessary power, and partly because the segments have chosen to exercise their influence on their own. The result, as the staff director for the Council complained in 1968, is that "it appears that "orderly growth" has been going forward on three fronts rather than one, permitting certain undesirable situations to develop."

Many problems thus still plague the system of higher education in California. It is faced with continued pressures to expand, both because of increasing numbers of students and because of continued internal competition among the segments. It is faced with an exceptional situation of budgetary stringency that has lasted for almost five years and promises to continue for several more years. And, because of campus turmoil in the middle and late 1960s, the political agencies in the state continue to be ambivalent about supporting the system. In the face of these problems and the existence of co-ordinating machinery that is voluntary and ineffective, it is not surprising that attempts to modify or even discard the co-ordinating machinery have been evident in the past decade. In 1965 the Legislature, dissatisfied with what it regarded as "bloc voting" by the different segments on the Co-ordinating Council, increased the number of public members from three to six, as a "balance" against the interests of the individual segments. In 1970 the Ways and Means Committee of the Assembly deleted the funds for the Co-ordinating Council for the forthcoming year. While the funds were partially restored subsequently, the act revealed the dissatisfaction of many legislators with the co-ordinating apparatus of the state's higher education system. And finally, early in 1971 the board's composition was once again changed, cutting the segments' representatives to four, leaving the public members at six, thus giving the public members a majority on the Council for the first time. As a result of these recent developments, the co-ordinating function for higher education has, like so many other issues in contemporary California, become infused by state politics.

California's system of higher education appears to be nearing the apex of one of its periodic crises of growth, governance, competition, and co-ordination. Its growth and its internal struggles have clearly exceeded the capacities of the voluntary co-ordinating machinery that was created by the Master Plan in 1960. The Co-ordinating Council's very existence has come into question; new plans for regional systems of integration and a comprehensive superboard have been advanced by leading political figures in the state; and two separate investigating groups—a subcommittee of the Co-ordinating Council and a joint committee of the two houses of the California Legislature—are undertaking a comprehensive review of the Master Plan. California history in the early 1970s appears to promise a period of vigours partisan struggle, search for new ideas, and institutional invention designed to contain its wonderful but somewhat wild educational system.

New—York The State University

The hunger of the American people for more and more education has become a dramatic phenomenon of our national life. Census figures compiled in 1970 reveal that the percentage of students graduating from secondary schools is now *double* the 1960 figure. During this same time period the percentage graduating from colleges and universities has *tripled*. And there is very little likelihood that this trend will level off before the 1980s.

What part has the State of New York played in satisfying the hunger of its citizens? In population it is the second largest of all the states; and it is the most affluent. For more than two centuries it was blessed with a steadily increasing number of excellent private colleges and universities, large and small, which met the major undergraduate and graduate educational needs. It also had a group of publicly supported undergraduate colleges in New York City that achieved considerable academic eminence. After World War II, however, it became clear that the total need was not going to be met without the development of a state university together with a large number of two-year community colleges. So rapidly has this development taken place that today, only a quarter of a century later, more than one-half of college and university students in the state are attending *public* institutions. By the end of this decade it is expected that the publicly supported colleges and universities will take care of three-fourths of the students.

The 1970 census figures help to explain why *public* higher education, which ordinarily makes provision for greater number of students than does private education, has become such a dominant force today. They also explain in part the extraordinary rapid growth of the State University of New York. Even though this is the youngest state university in the nation—having been established in 1948—it is already listed as the largest. In 1970 it enrolled more than 200,000 full-time students. More important than size, however, is the recognization that the university has become steadily more prominent for its developing academic quality and its unique form of organization.

The motto of the State University of New York is a clear statement of its philosophy: "Let Each Become All He Is Capable of Being." Such a commitment has had profound influence upon the organizational structure and the academic programs of the institution. What kind of university has emerged from such a motto?

Characteristics of the State University

There are three fundamental characteristics of the State University of New York. One of these is unique, the second is unusual, and the third you would expect to find in any first-rate academic institution.

The unique characteristic is that of a university embracing *all* the aspects and levels of higher education and thus being a system as much as a single institution. It comprises 69 separate campuses at the present time, with more in the planning stages. These run the gamut from university centres (where most of the graduate and professional work is concentrated), all the way to the two-years community or junior colleges in which it is possible for a student to start his post-secondary education close to his home. In between are arts and sciences colleges that offer the baccalaureate degree, specialized colleges such as forestry of ceramics or even preparation for careers in the maritime service, and agricultural and technical colleges.

The unusual characteristic is that of a decentralized method of operation linked to centralized guidance in philosophy and policy so that a feeling of university unity prevails. This means that each campus, although guided and governed by general policies of the university, has considerable independence in handling its own affairs. It has its own president and administration, its own board of trustees with designated responsibilities, its own budget, and its own identity as a separate institution within the university. At the same time, as part of the total university, each campus draws upon the central administration for assistance and guidance and upon the university Board of Trustees for broad policy decisions. Each campus also draws upon the special strengths of other campuses and often develops with them cultural of educational events or programs that it could not support by itself.

The third characteristic; which you would expect to find in any good university, is that of an institution with high aspirations and huge responsibilities moving steadily toward the finest quality in all that it attempts. Because it is located in a state famous for its excellent colleges and universities, the State University has had to strive with unusual intensity and speed to achieve an academic standard equal to the best. This has meant recruiting new faculty—including some of the finest scholars of the world—at the rate of more than a thousand annually. It has meant new buildings and equipment of all kinds, including the most sophisticated laboratories, computers, art galleries, theatres, and even completely new campuses. The current building program of the State University, involving a total outlay of more than three billion dollars, is the largest program of its kind in the world. Most of all, this effort toward high quality has meant the introduction of a whole host of new academic programs and a massive development of research activity.

Philosophy of the State University

I think I should say a further word about the educational philosophy on which all of this rests. When the State University asserts that each person should become "all he is capable of being", it is making a mighty assertion, one not to be taken lightly. It is saying that it plans its future in accordance with the philosophy of *full opportunity* for every individual, regardless of age, current occupation, previous educational accomplishments or status in life. To each person who can benefits from more education, the university aims to provide what he requires. This is a commitment in the true tradition of democracy, not an easy one to fulfil completely, but certainly one worth striving for. It means new and increased attention to individual guidance, new kinds of courses and programs to meet all sorts of needs, new kinds of testing procedures to determine what capabilities each person has. It means the acceptance of the relatively new concept that every student should proceed at his own speed of progress. It truly makes education a lifetime process with many of the traditionally formal barriers removed.

The State University of New York has always expressed its belief in this philosophy but only in the past few years has it taken bold steps to make certain that full opportunity would become a practical reality as well as a democratic dream. Last year, through the use of a variety of academic and administrative devices. It was able to open 14,000 additional places for students on its various campuses. This was over and above the normal student complement of the entering class. Just recently the university announced the establishment of its seventieth institution, to be devoted entirely to providing programs and examinations for students who cannot be in residence but who may now find it possible to earn one of a number of external degrees. These are dramatic illustrations of the unremitting efforts the university is making to assure the citizen of New York State of how seriously it takes its responsibility to provide a full educational opportunity for them.

Earlier, in mentioning the State University's motto, I asked what kind of institution has emerged. In answering this question, I have already identified three major characteristics that form the basic foundation on which the university is building: the unity of an institution that has within it all the diverse elements of higher education; the decentralized pattern of administration that protects local campus autonomy; the steadfast, unrelenting drive tiward high academic quality. These I should like to clarify even more by adding examples of each that may in their combined effect give you something of the flavor or the atmosphere of this university.

As a multicampus institution, the State University is more than the sum of its parts. Each campus has its own destiny to fulfil but in doing so, contributes not only to its sister campuses but to the single entity which is called the university. There is thus an interplay or interchange of strength constantly taking place between campuses and a process of unification that enriches the mother institution together with the offspring. The elements of this process become evident in many ways as we examine how the university operates.

Single Budget

For example, the total annual operating budget of the university (which is approximately one-half billion dollars) naturally must be presented for approval to the State Legislature, which has final approval and appropriates the money. You can well imagine what a complicated exercise this is. Think of how infinitely more complicated it would be if each of the 69 campuses were to present it own budget separately, without any regard for other campuses. Not only would an unproductive sort of competition be created, together with endless bickering among legislators who were eager to encourage the progress of only those campuses where their constituents lived, but no general educational pattern for the public sector could be developed over the years. In addition, it would be virtually impossible to avoid a large amount of unnecessary program duplication. For these reasons the State University presents a single budget for all its necessities and defends or explains any one of its items with as much detail as the legislature requests. Once the money has been appropriated, each campus thereafter had its own portion which it administers with a very high degree of independence.

Campus Interchange

Interchange and unification take place in many other ways, some more dramatic that others, but all of them important in the creation of a first class university.

Increasingly the library acquisitions of each campus are being made available to students on other campuses. This is now done mainly by the physical transfer of books and periodicals, but eventually will be done electronically and thus much more speedily. With total holdings of over 7,500,000 items already, the university is able to provide a wealth of library resources. Slowly but steadily the university is creating ways for its campuses to share such wealth for the benefit of every student and faculty member. The important point I making is that the unified university structure makes this kind of sharing much easier.

In addition to library resources there are many other types of resources shared within the university by its many campuses.

Regional computer centres—far beyond the financial capability of any single campus—are available to campuses as a group. These centres are used not only for academic work but for many administrative data processing functions that bring efficiency and economy to highly complicated and expensive operations.

A very different kind of educational and cultural activity that is strengthened by the presence of a multicampus university is that of the fine and performing arts. Like so many other academic institutions, the individual campuses of the State University offer such to the students in theatre, dance, film, music, or the fine and plastic arts, including instruction and studio work. But an important or even indispensable component of this kind of learning is that of seeing and hearing the finest of artists and their work. This component is not easy for each campus to make available, mainly because of cost. The State University provides such a component by having major orchestras, dance and theatre groups, exhibits, lectures, and artists-in-residence visit many of its campuses. Because of the number of such events it schedules in touring arrangements, it can make the whole venture far more economical to each campus. Still another component is the opportunity for students to view or hear the work of their peers. This they do through arts festivals and workshops where campuses merge their talents, sharpen their critical qualities, and acquire new perspectives by taking note of what others are doing.

In still another area, that of developing new educational resources for instruction, the university has taken advantage of its unified structure while at the same encouraging the independent action of the campuses. Many of the campuses have what are called "Communications-Lecture" buildings with several sizes of classrooms, television studios, audio-visual materials laboratories, and film libraries. All the communication media are used in a variety of combinations. For example, complete courses of instruction by television are created. These are often used on more than one campus according to the needs and desires of individual departments. In addition, the *University of the Air,* a television network, offers courses for credit or non-credit throughout the State of New York where each year from three to five thousand people avail themselves of this kind of external opportunity.

Support of research within the State University is administered through a special agency known as the Research Foundation, which handles more than $50 million of expenditures annually, most of which is derived from external grants. Through the resources of the Foundation the research activities of faculty members on all campuses are encouraged by individual grants to finance their projects. Almost a thousand such grants were made last year, with the selection of the recipients carried out by a faculty committee. Here is another illustration of the additional strength brought about by university unity in establishing and supporting a general policy while the practical effects reach out to the campuses and are controlled by them.

I could add much more documentation to the way campus independence and university unity are used to mutual advantage. I have said nothing, for example, about inter-campus faculty relations or student relations, nor have I mentioned community relations. The combination of unity and local autonomy is a difficult one to operate under successfully all the time, but it is the key to the growing ability of the State University to fulfil its enormous responsibilities.

University Planning

There is one other aspect of the university's development that cannot be omitted if you are to have a more complete understanding of what prompts and stimulates whatever happens within the institution. I am referring to the all-important process of planning.

Two kinds of planning are taking place at the State University, one required by legislative statute and the other a series of voluntary actions by the institution itself.

By law the university is obligated to submit a ten-years master plan every four years which then becomes part of the total Master Plan for higher education for the State. In addition, it is expected to make an annual report on progress in carrying out the master plan. The plan covers every aspect of academic and physical growth, together with estimates of enrollment and costs. It is therefore worked out in the greatest detail and is put together only after systematic consultation with each campus, each of which is asked to formulate its own plan. The plan thus serves as the basis for the future development of the university.

I cannot emphasize too strongly the importance of this regularized planning process, since it makes necessary not only a careful examination of present programs but places priorities on improvements and on the introduction of new programs, the establishment of additional colleges, and the introduction of innovative elements of education.

In an event broader way, the university is undertaking a reexamination of its own role and its aims. To do this it has created a Chancellor's Panel on University Purposes. The panel consists of representatives of trustees, administration, faculty, students, governmental officials, and distinguished citizens from all over the state. It strives to search deeply into the relivance of the university to the society it serves and to issue a series of statements that make clear the directions the university expects to take during the next two decades. Position papers are written and debated, discussions on campuses are organized to reflect internal attitudes and reactions, and outside experts are called in to react and advise. All this is being done not merely to create a statement that seems valid today but to maintain a continuing concern for changing needs and requirements.

What such an exercise will mean ultimately is hard to predict. It may lead to a completely new structure, a whole set of academic directions, an entirely different sort of relationship between the university and the community. I need not dwell upon the amount of work that goes into this kind of planning process; it is obviously difficult, time-consuming, and intellectually demanding. I can say only that in my view it is probably the single most worthwhile effort on which the university is embarked.

The surprising and exciting fact to be noted, in what I have described to you, is that all that has happened represents only the threshold for the development of the State University. In spite of the size, the growing prestige, and the many complicated arrangements by which it functions, it is truly only beginning to realize its potential. The university's comparative youth is a great asset when we consider such a potential. As an institution it is not so encrusted with tradition that change is extraordinarily difficult. It has a freshness about it, a sense of developing mission, an intellectual vitality that give it courage and lift not only its sights but its spirit as well. If it can continue to nurture such attitudes and turn them into intelligent, fearless actions, this university may well stand as on of the academic models that make the future of higher education more promising and more attractive.

The Drive for Co-ordination

Higher education is in a state of transaction. Under the pressures of increased numbers of students and rapidly rising costs, new organizations are being created that are changing the educational landscape. The traditional independence and autonomy of institutions is giving way to state or national co-ordinating bodies. In many countries this has led to increased governmental participation in the affairs of universities and colleges. These new systems, of which the university is simply a part, from a structure of higher education that has so far been largely unexamined. In this series of lectures we hope to illuminate, for the first time, the ways in which systems are being developed to provide for planning and co-ordination of higher education. Since many countries are struggling with similar problems in the effort to bring planning to their educational systems, the presentation will be inter-national in scope.

I would like first to review briefly the factors behind the drive for planning and co-ordination. Most educators are all too familiar with the multiplicity of crises facing their institutions. In the last two decades we have seen growth in higher education that can only be called phenomenal. Enrollment has doubled, tripled, or quadrupled in many countries. Thus the physical expansion of our institutions of higher education became inevitable; schools grew larger and larger, and many new campuses were established.

The so-called knowledge explosion created a different kind of strain on traditional institutions. Where the university had once thought off itself as an institution that could explore the unity of knowledge, it now finds that in order to maintain excellence it must concentrate on specialized segments of knowledge. In the past decade or so, new kinds of schools—two-year colleges, teacher training institutes, technical institutes—have emerged in many countries; so also have new uses to technology, such as educational television. The growing and special needs for higher education seemingly can no longer be met in a uniform system.

As colleges and universities have become more specialized, they have also become interdependent. The distinguished scientist Caryl Haskins has provided a useful model for the study of organisms and organizations. I think this model applies particularly to the development of higher education. In his book *Of Societies and Men* he relates how growth leads to complexity, complexity to specialization, and specialization to integration. When we look at higher education, we can see that the need for co-ordination of our specialized institutions is one of the prime reasons for the development of systems.

The towering costs of our academic enterprises are another element in the drive for co-ordination. Area studies programs require more and more hard-to-get books, and their personnel, more and more airplane tickets; the physics laboratory requires an incredibly costly electron microscope; the college of agriculture requires an expensive computer to keep track of the health of the cattle in its region. No university could assume the expense of all these facilities itself. Moreover, the high level of expertise needed for all these activities is just not available on any single campus.

Another trend has become unmistakable. Because the costs of higher education are so enormous, there has been growing reliance on public funds for support. Dependence on public funds has led, in turn, to increased demands for accountabilty to the public or governmental authority. In the past, in countries where higher education was formerly supported largely through private means, there was less public scrutiny of how an institution used its resources. That has all changed. Now we see a critical concern for achieving balance between the needs for funding, planning, and co-ordination on the one side, and the needs for independence, freedom to innovate, and internal flexibility on the other.

The need for planning has given further impetus to authorities outside the university. With the rising clamor for admission to higher education, attended by an equal clamor for trained manpower, no political body at any level can afford to allow the public's great interest in educational development to be satisfied by mere chance.

Now let us examine for a moment the hierarchy of institutions that are being developed in higher education. This new world is fascinating to behold, it is almost like watching islands rise out of the sea in response to subterranean upheavals. Some systems have been designed to co-ordinate the interest of the universities: The University Grants Committee in Great Britain functions in this way, acting as intermediary between universities and the government. Others have been designed to bridge the state-federal relationship, such as the Wissenschaftsrat in West Germany. Still others leave most of their planning and co-ordination to the central ministry of education, as in Sweden and Japan. All these systems, however, are faced with the same problems of how to harmonize the interest of students, faculties, administrators, governments, and the general public.

Systems in the United States

I would like now to outline the complicated picture of systems in the United States, which will be covered in detail by the next few speakers in this series. Later speakers will be describing systems that have emerged in other countries. In the final lecture of the series I will try to pull together our observations on the future of co-ordination.

In the United States it was natural that the first efforts at developing higher education would take place at the state level. Public higher education has always been essentially a state responsibility in America. Therefore, it was the governors and state legislators, with their political sensitivities, who first presented demands for state plans and for institutions to carry them out. In the American tradition, the solutions have varied from one state to the next.

But even statewide plans and statewide administrative systems have not met all the needs. For example, the existence of comparable and expensive professional schools in adjacent states was found to be both inefficient and extravagant. In the interest of sharing resources, state governments and universities have banded together to form regional organizations based on interstate compacts. The Southern Regional Education Board, the Western Interstate Compact for Higher Education, and the New England Board of Higher Education, the major regional organizations in the United States, thus emerged.

Not all regional organizations are of the state compact type. Nor do all of them involve the direct participation of public authorities. In the Midwest, for example, the universities themselves have banded together to from the Committee on Institutional Co-operation, consisting of the "Big Ten" and the University of Chicago. In this case, the universities, not the state governments, took the initiative; even more uniquely, this committee involves the equal participation of both public and private institutions.

Useful as organization at the regional level are in the United States, they frequently suffer from being suspended between the two focal points of real political power—the state and the federal governments. Although the federal government has traditionally not had a direct responsibility for education, this situation is in the process of dramatic change. Perhaps predictably, this change has followed rather than preceded the development of a national view-point on the part of educators. Let us look briefly at some of the present pieces of such a national system.

The first structure were, naturally enough, a series of associations of colleges and universities organized to exchange views about common problems. These associations have prospered and multiplied. Today they cover, on a national basis, every conceivable type and style of college and university. Even within this welter of associations, the instinct for order has asserted itself with the formation of the American Council on Education as the top holding company for all the special groups, ranging from the American Alumni Council to the Association of American Colleges.

Then there are the great foundations with both national and international programs. Committed to spending their incomes wisely for new ventures, they must develop ideas of the national interest in education as guides to giving. And they do. But these ideas of the national interest, even though completely unco-ordinated, serve to impress on the national community images of national purpose and national priorities that work their way into the plans and programs of public and private agencies. It is not just through their grants that the foundations exercise their influence, but also through the design and strategies that determine their grants. Foundations serve, therefore, as national planners in the private educational sector, even though the effects of their plans may not always be decisive.

Another segment of our national educational superstructure consists of the agencies that have been created to perform various functions that the universities could not perform individually and never did perform collectively. The need for a broadly based faculty retirement program, for example, which made it possible for a professor to take his pension with him from one institution to the next, led to the creation of the Teachers Insurance and Annuity Association at the end of the First World War. Similarly, the need for national program of testing for the admission of students to higher education led to the College Entrance Examination Board and the Educational Testing Service. The desire for national scholarship and fellowship programs, which would recognize the national distribution of talent, led to the Woodrow Wilson Fellowship Program and the National Merit Scholarship Corporation. And a mounting concern over the international aspects of higher education, including the development of higher education abroad, led to the formation of the Institute of International Education, the African-American Institute, and more recently, the International Council for Educational Development.

Each of these organizations has been established to perform special tasks for higher education, but significantly all of them have been organized at the instance of some source outside the university world. It is a sober thought that the universities have not had the imagination or the initiative to establish these agencies themselves. Meanwhile, these agencies are in a rather strange position: they are under the supervision neither of the university nor of any other educational authority, except the ad-hoc boards that were created to run them or the foundations that came up with the ideas and provided the original funds.

Activities of great importance to the universities are thus now completely outside their control. But it is well to note that the system as a whole is still in transition. Sooner or later, either new concepts and structures will emerge that will embrace both the universities and these service organizations or else the universities may decide to supervise the job themselves, as perhaps they should have done all along.

Role of Federal Government

Behind all these private organizations, of course, stands the presence of the federal government—increasingly committed to the improvement of educational opportunity, to the strengthening of institutions of secondary and higher education, to the encouragement of higher standards of performance, to the advancement of research required in the national interest, to an expansion of the creative arts, and to a concern for educational development in modernizing countries. An aroused government is thus responding on many fronts to a sharpened conception of the national interest in education.

But the role of the federal government as co-ordinator and manager has yet to be brought into focus. Since the federal government has not had prime responsibility for education in the United States, the lag is understandable. But assistance is now coming from many federal sources, and other signs of an expanding federal interest are not hard to find. Questions of educational standards have already been raised by the government. And vigorous federal attention is being given to problems ranging from the education of the disadvantaged and the quality of urban schools to medical education and the better distribution of university excellence throughout the country. This expanding federal role puts the most severe pressure on the public and private universities to evolve national organizations and programs of their own that will act is both counterparts and counterweights to the new federal interest.

International Agencies

Moving with a perspective even broader than that of the federal government, meanwhile, are those agencies busy with higher education at the international level. There are international regional bodies, such as the Union of Latin American Universities, the Council of Southeast Asia

Universities, the new Association of African Universities, and the Carnegic-sponsored Council on Higher Education in the American Republics. And there are such universal bodies as the public Unesco and the private International Association of Universities.

Although many of these groups are relatively new—and some are still quite—fragic—they are beginning to monitor a variety of important studies that may well affect planning at national, regional, state, and even university levels, particularly in the area of assistance to universities in the underdeveloped countries. As a sense of world community evolves, and increasingly it must, these international agencies will be in ever stronger positions to express their interests and to influence educational planning.

That is roughly the picture of the educational pyramid that is now emerging. The university is only one level in the whole vast hierarchy of education that has been built up around it. Below it are the department and the college, and the complex of liberal arts and technical schools. Above it are the state agencies, the regional organizations, the federal structures, and finally the international organizations. Each of these organizations, arranged one on top of the other, represents a new interest at a new and larger geographical level.

In the long run, this structure itself matters very little to society as a whole. What society cares about is not which level of this hierarchy has the right to lead and to make decisions. What matters is that the right decisions are made at the level most competent to make them, and that these decisions are carried out successfully. The approval of society will come, in the end, not by claims of privilege but rather from results observed over time. And the desired results will be in those areas where society asks the most of its educational systems.

Critical Role of University

Let us look at several of the requirements that society imposes on education and examine the capabilities of the various levels to deal with them. For what we find here will give us an important clue to the distribution of power and, not least, to the crucial role of the university in the entire educational organization.

First, let us look at the protection of academic freedom, for without academic freedom there is no educational system worth discussing. Again my remarks are directed mainly to the system in the United States, although many of the same considerations apply elsewhere.

The department and the college within the university are important for organizing the defense of freedom; but since they do not have the legal authority to hire and fire, they obviously cannot do the job alone. The university faculty is even more important, first, because it can speak more easily for the university as a whole, and second, because it is the body that participates in setting the rules of tenure.

Important as the faculty is in the protection of academic freedom, however, clearly the real defense within the university comes from the joining of trustees, administration, and faculty. It is a simplistic and outdated notion that working together with trustees and administration results in compromise of academic freedom. As a matter of fact, in the overwhelming majority of cases, faculties, administrations, and trustees have developed a solid consensus on the subject of academic freedom, and scholars are well protected by it.

Beyond the university, concern for academic freedom weakens as move up the scale. It is not that regional and international bodies aren't interested; it is simply that they know they can't do anything about academic freedom, so they are concentrating on other matters. They assume that the universities are responsible for academic freedom and have the power to defend it. We can conclude, therefore, that the unique combination of forces at the level of the university provides the greatest barrier to the violation of academic freedom.

A second fundamental requirement posed for an educational system is the need for continuous change and innovation. The world is obviously faced with a vast need for new ideas and for manpower trained in new areas of knowledge. Let us see how change is regarded at each level of the hierarchy we have just described.

Again, let us start with the department. A relatively flexible instrument when compared with the great professor in universities abroad who dominates his field, the department is in most cases essentially a conservative-unit. Its actions and positions reflect its dominant elements and the forces that have been balanced to produce some kind of department consensus. Those who make the consensus are not likely to produce the revolution to upset it. Furthermore, departments are not easily subject to change from the outside. They have become specialized in their fields of knowledge to the point where faculty from other departments find it very difficult to recommend changes, even when they have a vague feeling that changes are in order. Professional specialization frequently cuts so deep that faculty in one specially are not in the best position to see into the next academic channel. All of this makes change at the department level somewhat hard to come by.

At the level of the collegiate dean, innovation can be accomplished, but it is a delicate art. For the dean who wishes to exercise leadership,the task of innovation will be easier if he has arranged for the rotation of departmental chairmen. He can also wield great influence by concentrating his attention on filling the major vacancies with men of the highest professional quality and by keeping to those occasions when the time is ripe for improvement.

The same prescriptions apply to the university president, although, generally speaking, his access to funds gives him an even more powerful lever in effecting change. It is a lever, however, that he must employ the care. He must not allow the availability of funds to become more important than the changes they are to bring about. A president is, or should be, in touch both with new requirements and with new ideas, and if he cannot bring them to the attention of his community, he abdicates his academic leadership.

Outside the university, the various co-ordinating bodies have great potential as innovating forces. So far, however, the performance of supra-university groups as agents of change has not been impressive. The regional compact organizations have to keep fighting a tendency to the routine. Perhaps, they feel too directly the weight of public bureaucracy, or perhaps they are too new to have achieved the necessary acceptance. The voluntary organizations, notably the Committee on Institutional Co-operation, appear to have more zest and imagination.

Foundations

The most vigorous agents for innovation are the great private foundations and federal agencies, such as the National Institutes of Health, the National Science Foundation, and the U.S. Office of Education. These federal agencies have the great advantage of being free from the direct operations that restrict the range and vision of many state educational offices. Further, the new money continually available for new ideas makes federal agencies for the foreseeable future, at least—extremely powerful forces for change and modernization. We are perhaps too dimly aware of the blessings of a system that leaves the federal government free to press for improvement and change, while the states bear the burden of daily operating supervision and budget making. This freedom, it seems to me, is the most persuasive argument for having the federal government stay away from assuming direct responsibility. I hope that federal officials will not overlook this advantage.

The role of the foundations as innovators has been crucial, particularly at the program level. It is unlikely that major new programs in U.S. institutions, such as area studies, the new mathematics, and honours courses, would have gone into such speedy academic orbit if foundation initiative and foundation backing had not been available. But foundation funds, with the exception of those of the Ford Foundation, are becoming a smaller and smaller fraction of the total academic budget. The tendency will be for foundations to move away from institution-wide support and even from programs and projects, and finally to become operating institutions that use their income for their own internal programs. Since the budget for higher education is increasing faster than the income of foundations, foundation support can be expected to play less of a direct part in educational change. The effect of these developments will be to shift the source of the innovative force from foundations to federal agencies on the program and project level.

Planning

A third area of public interest in the university system has to do with planning. The significant point about planning is that, as the cost and importance of educational matters increase, decision-making moves up the hierarchical scale, and away from the educational institutions toward political structures.

It is only half the story to say that management and decision-making go up the scale as costs and importance of a project increase. The other half is that, as costs and importance rise, there is a tendency for decision-making to gravitate closer to the political arena. The decision to locate a 10-billion-electronic-volt machine at Cornell University was a budget decision made at the level of the White House. It very nearly became a deeper political question involving the Senate and other regions of the country. The whole matter was a fascinating case study of the impact of cost and size on the locus of decision-making.

The raises a final point about planning. If planning now requires the participation of larger and more comprehensive organizations, then universities will have to modify their instincts for autonomy and take their places as full partners in these new planning agencies. If they do not, the motivable consequence will that planning and co-ordination will be performed by an exclusively political body.

This is the complicated balance of considerations facing all systems of higher education. The price of too much decentralization is to create an administrative vacuum within the education hierarchy—a vacuum which will inevitably be filled by political authority. Too little decentralization keeps the central power in academic hands, but the price may be paralysis on individual campuses. It requires considerable statesmanship to understand clearly the dangers of either extreme solution.

Those who want academic direction to remain in academic hands have no choice. It seems to me, but to learn how to balance their desires for independence with the necessities for close collaboration with other universities. The only alternative will be a far more direct intervention in university affairs by government agencies. And none of us looks comfortably on that prospect.

University Retains Decisive Role

Finally, we must mention the responsibility for the integration of teaching, research, and public service—the traditional missions of higher education in the United States. Has any agency above the level of the university established a claim to perform this task better than the university? The answer is clearly no. The specialized agencies have important roles to play in helping the university to find answers to one or another of its activities or requirements. But testing, faculty pensions, student mobility, fellowships and scholarships, co-ordination, planning, and the stimulation of change—none of these activities is as central to the management of knowledge as is the essential work of the university. The university remains one level in the new educational hierarchy—but it is the decisive level.

The moral of our story is that the university's role demands not isolation but leadership, not autonomy but rather participation in all levels of academic organization. As the one institution in the hierarchy of education where the main business of education is centred, the university must be the chief participant, the quarter back, the leader in the whole system of higher education. For the health of the system turns largely on the vitality and health of the university, located in the middle of the entire scheme. And in order to maintain the university's vitality, those who work in the university must increasingly conduct themselves as members of a much larger community and as participants in activities at all levels of the system.

5

Education in Malaysia

A high-level manpower survey, on the lines used in this report, is in process of completion in Malaya and some provisional results have been obtained. These results are used here in their crude form; but the further work which is being done will refine them. There is a good link between manpower work and educational planning through the Higher Education Planning Committee, and some (but not enough) linkage between that committee and the over-all economic planning for Malaysia. This machinery, if it can be kept working, and accelerated, should provide a good basis for policy making in both the economic and, more particularly, the whole field of higher education. This report is concerned primarily with four key sectors—agriculture, industrialization, health and education. The construction industry, which is another sector of growing importance, would require a specialized study of its own.

THE ECONOMY

Population

From the 1957 census, the 'medium' fertility rate projection of population growth provided by the Census Department is:

	Malaysian	*Chinese*	*Indian*	*Other*	*All races*
1962	3,709,000	2,771,000	843,000	140,000	7,463,000
1967	4,381,000	3,282,000	1,014,000	154,000	8,831,000
1972	5,158,000	3,888,000	1,220,000	—	10,450,000
1982	7,130,000	5,502,000	1,851,000	—	14,703,000

The United Nations population median projection, for slightly different periods gives slightly lower total figures (all races); 1960, 6,965,000; 1965, 8,131,000; 1970, 9,499,000; 1980, 13,078,000. These figures assume an annual growth of 3.1 per cent (1960-65) to 3.3 per cent (1975-80). For purposes of high-level manpower calculations these differences are not greatly significant, and it is clear that rounded figures of 7 millions, 1960; 8 million, 1965; and 9.5 million, 1970, will not be far out.

General Economic Growth Problems

During the last few years Malaya has been pushing ahead with a bold development programme while suffering a quite steep fall in the price of her biggest export, rubber. The key figures reflect this. Physical production has been growing, at rather more than 4 per cent per annum. But when the figures are translated into money terms, the fall in rubber prices has dragged the indices down. The effects are shown in value of *per capita* income, and in a large and possibly growing deficit both in the current budget and in the balance of payments. Development expenditure in the second half of the decade will be largely deficit spending.

In general, it is hoped to offset the expected continuation of fall in rubber prices by high total yields and higher yields per acre, so that the total value of the crop recovers to about MS 1,500 million by 1970 even on a price per pound of only 55 cents. Meanwhile, tin production has been increasing and tin prices have soared to boom levels, which helps to offset the loss on rubber. Deficits will have to be financed by foreign capital investment in industry, and by running down foreign reserves and increasing internal savings. The economy will go through a period of fairly acute strain, but it should be manageable, provided that defence expenditure does not have to rise too steeply.

In manpower terms, it is the investment side of the economy which matters. Provided that the deficits can be financed, development expenditure which has risen so steeply implies a heavy call on high-level manpower for technical services, supervision and administration. At lower levels, however, total employment respondents more sluggishly to investment, and in 1962 the economy showed about 6 per cent of unemployment. This is not a disastrous figure, but it could be serious in social terms. Industry unfortunately absorbs all too little labour per unit of capital invested; the main hope of expanding total employment will be in raising the standards of living in the whole dispersed economy, generating a large number of jobs in rural areas and small country towns and settlements. Particular attention is therefore, given in this report to land, agricultural and rural development.

TABLE 5.1

Economic indices

Index	1960	1961	1962	1963	1960/1962
Gross domestic Product (1959 dollars) (M.$ million)	5191	5458	5672		% 109.3
Gross nationalproduct (market prices) (M.$ million)	5665	5604	5786		102.1
GNP per capita (M.$ million)	819	783	785		95.8
Actual develoopment expenditure (M.$ million)	201.4	350.5	544.9	600[2]	
Balance of payments (current account) M.$ million)	+308	+14	-203	-209[2]	

Federal budget (surplus or deficit) (M.$ million)	+100	-70	-170	-370[2]
Rubber price (cents per lb.)	108.1	83.5	78.2	
Rubber production (000 tonns)	708	737	751	770
Rubber value (M.$ million)	1691	1346	1298	
All races retail price indes (1959 = 100)	99.8	99.6	99.7	101.6[2]

1. The figures are from Interim Review of Development in Malaya under the Second Five-Year Plan (Kuala Lumpur, December 1963).
2. Extimate.
3. July 1963.

In a broad sense, it sill not be easily possible to continue the rise in physical output (which demands physical effort) without an accompanying rise in income per head, i.e., some real reward in purchasing power for the mass of people. Retail prices have remained remarkably steady, which is a good women. Further, the ordinary man will be getting much improved social and environmental services—more education for his children, better roads and so on. But these cost money in the budget and are apt to be taken for granted by the consumer. Increased personal purchasing power will mean a higher GNP per head in terms not merely of infrastructure but of increased personal earnings.

It is clear that if the rubber programme maintains the value of output over some years, despite falling prices positive growth in national income will have to come from other sectors. The two most likely are increased and diversified production of non-rubber crops: rice, palm oil, coconut, pineapple, tobacco, animal industry; and the industrial sector. It is also implied that very heavy capital investment on long dated schemes—such as the FLDA land settlements, which give virtually no return to the settlers for five or six years—may add to the strain on the economy without any revenue or incentive effect through the most critical period.

THE EDUCATIONAL SYSTEM

Primary

Enrollments (1962): total primary, 1,133,269; standard I,223,552; standard VI, 173,136; percentage of VI to I,77.4.

Total by streams: English, 229,339; Malay, 487,246; Chinese, 354,366; Indian, 62,318; total 1,133,269.

The survival rate of entrants to standard I in 1956 to numbers in standard VI in 1961 was 74.75 per cent; it has greatly improved over the last seven years.

Secondary

Enrollments (1962); total secondary, 202,368; form 1,60,008; form 5,16,525; form 6(1), 1,132; form 6(2), 990.

Total by streams: English, 156,463; Malay, 14,534; Chinese, 31,371; total 202,368.

Two separate estimates give the following rates of survival through secondary education:

1,000 boys and 1,000 girls enter form 1;

550 boys and 640 girls survive to form 4 after climinating examination at form 3;

198 boys and 282 girls survive to form 6(1) after School Certificate at form 5;

147 boys and 200 girls survive to university entrance after Higher School Certificate at form 6(2).

Survival rate = 17.35 per cent.

The survival rate from form 5 to form 6 appears in practice to be considerably lower. For example, in 1962 from 6,119 entries to the form 6 entry examination, only

964 were assured of places (16.6 per cent) and 330 extra qualified for 'provisional' places, making a total of 22 per cent. This contrasts with the 40 per cent survival from form 5 to form 6(1) suggested above. The Ministry of Education projections to 1977 are based on a survival rate from form 1 to form 6(2) of only 8 per cent.

University (Kuala Lumpur)

Total enrollment in 1962 was 1,331 (arts. 714; science, 317; engineering, 225; agriculture, 75). In that year 533 students were in their first year, so that not more than that number would graduate in 1965/66. Estimates of future enrollment total 2,612 in 1965 and 3,918 in 1968. Output of graduates for 1968 is estimated at 795.

SPECIAL REQUIREMENTS FOR HIGH-LEVEL MANPOWER

Agriculture

The strategic problems of agricultural development in Malaya are quite simply stated:

1. In the expectation of falling rubber prices, replanting of high-yielding varieties and extension of acreage (including land settlement of schemes) will be used to increase output so that total financial yield remains as stable as possible.
2. It is therefore imperative that other crops should be developed to provide for economic growth—this effort is directed partly to new commercial export crops (oil palm, etc.) and partly to food crops (double-cropping of rice, improvement of single crop yields, development of animal husbandry, fruit, vegetables, canning and processing industries).
3. This programme will involve both a rapid and massive extension of agricultural field staff, and equally a

large investment in research, especially on soils, varieties, crop and animal husbandry, and commercial/industrial techniques for processing and marketing: this involves expanding training at all levels.

In fact, Malaya is paying a price for over-concentration on rubber and a comparative neglect of the staff necessary to develop other crops.

The following figures for crop acreages in 1961 will illustrate the present position: rubber, 3,923,000; oil palm, 141,000; coconut, 439,867; paddy (all types), 932,000; fruit, 214,000 (pineapple, 42,000; durian 34,000; banana, 66,000; rambutan, 24,000); other food crops 136,000 (tapioca, 40,000); miscellaneous, 73,000 (nipah, 31,000; coffee, 16,700; tea, 4,5000; tobacco, 7,628); spices, 47,000; total 5,907,594. Thus roughly 4 million out of 6 million acres is devoted to rubber, and nearly I million acres to rice.

Meanwhile various estimates of food consumption per household show that average total calorie intake in Malaya is probably sufficient but that there are quite serious deficiencies in protective foods. Among the lowest income groups both calories and protective foods are short, the latter by as much as 50 per cent below an acceptable average.

Further, Malaya is spending heavily on food imports, including about 35 per cent of rice requirements.

TABLE 5.2

Major Food Imports, 1960

Sector	*Value, M.$ million*	*Percentage of total imports*
Rice	134.8	6.3
Milk products	99.6	4.5

Sugar, etc.	67.5	3.1
Fruit and vegetables	62.9	2.9
Wheat flour	60.8	2.9
Meat	32.1	1.5
Fish and fish preparations	28.3	1.3
Animal feeding stuffs	28.0	1.3
Other (beverages, tea, coffee, etc).	84.0	3.8
Total	598.0	27.8

Figures which are particularly striking, apart from rice, are fruit and vegetables, meat, fish and animal feeding stuffs, all capable of local production. Future difficulties in the balance of trade point strongly to local production in place of imports in these sectors. There is even some possibility of sugarcane production.

As to rice, the main effort is to extend double-cropping, chiefly in Province Wellesley, where master is available, but later in Kedah, where up to 100,000 acres could be handled when a major irrigation scheme is put in. In 1963 there were about 26,000 acres under double-cropping in Province Wellesley. The programme was set back by the introduction of a round-grained rice for the second crop which was unpopular with consumers; a new variety without this disadvantage is being developed. There is also, in Kelantan, the possibility of using tobacco as a second crop; the financial return to the grower is extremely attractive. The total area of double-cropped paddy is by 1964 probably around 45,000 acres. i.e., less than 5 per cent of all paddy acreage.

A major effort will be needed to develop other food and commercial crops, not only in the growing but in developing varieties suited to canning and market demand and uniform in quality; in replacing inefficient milling and processing methods, and in marketing.

There are also large opportunities for animal husbandry (cattle, pigs, poultry) and for growing fodder crops, notably the leguminous crop with which young rubber is in any case under-planted. The fact that animal husbandry is separated off from Agriculture to the Veterinary Department has made it difficult for agricultural extension workers to develop mixed farming.

In face of such a large, varied intensely interesting and hopeful programme of agricultural development, both the field and research staff have been wholly inadequate in numbers. In the Second Five-Year Plan, out of M.$545.3 million devoted to agricultural development, only M.$20 million was allocated to extension services and research. It is significant that from the same planning budget M.$166 million was allocated to rubber replanting and M.$91 million to land development.

The schemes of the Federal Land Development Authority (FLDA) have absorbed a huge proportion of money and effort. They have their own justification, in catching up with the war-time and emergency arrears of land alienation, in extending cultivable acreages, in providing land and employment to a small part of a growing population, and in providing a cash-crop to farmers of 10-acre holdings which are designed to give both vegetables, a fruit crop and a cash income of about £500 per annum per family when the rubber (or palm oil) is fully developed. By the end of 1963 schemes covering 200,000 acres, designed for 15,000 settler families were in hand, with nearly 70,000 acres of rubber planted out of 154,000 due for planting (30,000 to Dusun)—nearly 6,000 families were by then resident. The programme is for twelve schemes of 4,000 acres per annum, each settling 400 families. In view of the relatively small population which can be affected, the long-term nature of the yield (the families have to be paid subsistence as a loan until fruit and then rubber crops come into bearing), the need for more research on the minor crops in the scheme, the heavy financial strain on the Malayan economy during 1965-68 and the urgent need for investment in other types of agricultural development, it is questionable whether the balance of effort and investment is right. It should be added that land alienation and settlement is proceeding rapidly under less thorough-going schemes. Figures show 22,000 settlers and 92,000 acres planted under 'fringe alienation' and 12,000 settlers with 44,000 acres planted under 'controlled alienation'. The following proposals on manpower will assume that, in any case, the new investment inn diversification will take place, although in competition for funds with FLDA, and therefore that the additions to agricultural staff, which are essential for it, will be authorized.

This emphasis on crop diversification should not, however, overshadow the immense achievement of the rubber industry in driving the crop up to record figures (about 770,000 tons in 1963) and in replanting (about 500,000 acres of smallholder rubber have been covered since the replanting schemes were started). A milestone was passed when 3,000 Ib. of rubber was harvested from a single acre in 1963.

Detailed consideration has recently been given by the Government to the strength of the advisory and research staff, and decisions may be now have been reached. The suggested expansions are shown in Table 5.3.

At the graduate level, there are other branches with research and some field staff, of which the Rubber Research Institute and field staff are by far the most important.

TABLE 5.3

Suggested Establishment for Advisory and Research Staff

Category	*Div. I: agricultural officer, research officer, agronomist, etc.*		*Div. II: agricultural assistant, laboratory technician, etc.*		*Div. III: Junior agricultural assistant, laboratory assistant, etc.*	
	Present	New	Present	New	Present	New
Field staff	15	38	105	262	436	1,666
Research staff	48	199	59	398	200	1,194
Total	63	237	155	660	636	1,860

TABLE 5.4

Other Research and Field Staff

Branch	*Div. I*	*Div. II*	*Div. III*
Rubber Research Institute, etc. (1963)	101	31	180
Forest Research Institute'	12+		
Veterinary Research Institute headquarters (and field staff)	17	10	(?120)
Fishery research and field	17	(?40)	(?400)

1. Total forestry staff, 1960: Division I, 39; Division II, 37; Division III, 214; Division IV. 633

If these posts, all of which require biological background and applied training, are added to the new agricultural proposals, the result is: Division I, 384; Division II, 740; Division III, 3,260. This does not include the teaching and research staff at the university (about 20) and at Serdang, nor the forestry field staff. Nor does it allow for expansion in the Rubber Research Institute, and forestry, etc., staffs.

While Malaya certainly needs a large expansion of staff, these figures, and especially the agricultural figure, look somewhat high for a country of Malaya's population. The additions would, of course, be phased over a ten-years period.

Moreover, the figures are swollen by the inclusion of all research staff under 'agriculture', whereas in many countries they would appear under a university or special research institution. It is true that behind every graduate field officer there needs to be an output of at least three biological degrees, concerned with the whole agricultural field; and including research, teaching, marketing, processing, and commercial management (supply and services).

It will be clear (see below) that these total figures, with additions to the rubber and veterinary staff which are sure to be called for, cannot in any case be reached in five years from local output; the might quite reasonably be regarded as a fifteen-year target. It might be sensible to suggest, as a target for the early 1970s, the approximate figures given in Table 5.5 It would be time enough to review these figures in 1967, with a view to expansion, if necessary, in the decade 1970-80.

TABLE 5.5

Suggested Target for the 1970's

Category	*Div. I*	*Div. II*	*Div. III*
Field	40	260	1,250
Research	120	300	800
	160	560	2,050
Add:			
Rubber	120	60	300
Other, and teaching	70	100	150
Total	350	720	2,500

The annual outputs to maintain a force of this size in the field, assuming a 20-years life on the job (5 per cent p.a., wastage), would be 17 per annum for Division I. 36 per annum for Division II and 125 per annum for Division III.

In fact, however, since wastage is likely to be much higher in Division I owing to expatriates leaving on retirement and to the engagement of officers on short contracts, the wastage rate for Division I is likely to be far higher in the early stages. Moreover, these figures make no allowance for providing trained staff to the private sector, to processing and industrialized concerns in the food industry, and to new research units which will no doubt be developed. There will also be a drain of experienced diploma-level staff for management of FLDA settlement schemes, at a rate of about 12 new posts per annum. It would be reasonable to aim at an output of 35 per annum for Division 1,50 per annum for Division II and 120 per annum for Division III (where wastage is not likely to be so great). These figures are for maintenance only.

To reach the stock figures reasonably quickly requires, temporarily, a much higher output. This can no doubt be achieved for Division III, since facilities for training can be readily increased. Division II staff are trained at Serdang College of Agriculture, which has recently been expanded to take 120 students, with School Certificate entry. If the college can increase its output to 100 per annum by 1968-69, it should be possible at a later stage to devote some of the facilities to training a better level of Division III staff and to add a year to the diploma-level (Division II) course, thus reducing the candidates for Division II posts which, by 1970, might not absorb more than 50 per annum at most.

At the university level about 100 students in all were enrolled in 1963, providing a maximum output from the four-year courses of about that number by 1967-68. Thereafter, it should be possible to increase the output from the present faculty to about 35 per annum. Since a high proportion of research staff should come from the Faculty of Science (botany, zoology, chemistry, etc.), it would appear that, in the longer term, this output would be sufficient. But the faculty would certainly wish to develop, in association with the Science and Engineering faculties, a strong post-graduate school. In general, it would be a mistake to emphasize the first degree of the Agricultural Faculty as the dominant source of staff for agriculture. A very practical and high-quality college for field training at diploma level, first-rate departments of botany, zoology, chemistry, etc., in the university, good post-graduate schools and research institutes will, in the future, be just as essential as an output of B.Sc. (Agriculture) graduates.

In the meantime, quite extensive engagement of contract expatriates, and an expansion of scholarship programmes for local candidates will be needed.

TABLE 5.6

Suggested Levels of Output, Per Annum

	1970	*1975*
University		
Faculty of Agriculture, first degree	25-30	35
Faculty of Agriculture, post-graduate	10	15
Science Faculty, agricultural bias	70	100
Serdang College	100	50[1]
		50[2]
Division III training	200	100

1. Diploma three-year course.
2. Improved Division III two-year courses.

Engineering, Technical, Commercial, Management

Engineers. The 1963 Survey of Key Occupations listed 1,977 engineers in Category I; a high proportion of these would be expatriates at the present time. The University in

Kuala Lumpur had an output of just over 20 in 1962, estimated to rise to about 100 in 1968. The total produced over that period would be about 410. An output of 100 per annum would sustain a force of 2,500. The force of engineers should, however, rise fast over the next ten years, if possible 100 per cent by 1975, i.e., 4,000. Some engineers of professional level will come from the Technical College—perhaps one-fifth of its present total output of 100 students of all grades per annum. It is clear that no help can come from Singapore, where the facilities are fully engaged for its own needs; and eventually Malaya should be training professional engineers for Sabah and Sarawak, assuming that technicians will be trained on the island. An output of 200 engineering qualifications at professional level per year would seem a minimum target, to be realize as soon as possible. This is fact implies a new engineering school. It is true that the faculty in Kuala Lumpur will have an enrolment of 750-800 in 1968, and therefore an output of 150 or more in 1972. But this is about the limit of size, and the target will continue to rise.

Technicians. The 1963 survey lists 4,300 technicians on the industrial side, including pharmaceuticals, and 620 in survey, architectural drawing, town planning, printing and cartography—total, say, 5,000. This would require an annual output of 200 to maintain and of as much as 500 to increase to the levels required in the 1970s. At least one more full-scale technical college will be needed, assuming that the existing college in Kuala Lumpur can raise its output to 200 per annum, which should not be impossible, and that departmental schemes are maintained and increased. There would be a strong case for placing such a college in north-west Malaya—Ipoh or Penang.

In addition, more upgrading of artisans through technical evening classes could be organized in co-operation with industry. The scale of the new Ministry of Labour training centre in Kuala Lumpur might well make it worth while to use it for higher than artisan training, at least at night. Even with these additions, a third technical college may well have to be considered.

Architects, surveyors, quantity surveyors, town planners. At graduate level, 244 were listed in 1963. Malaya will presumably rely partly on overseas courses, and occasional students accepted in the Singapore course when it reaches professional level. The Technical College should be able to produce the necessary supply of Category II technicians and draughtsmen, and already produces architects up to the RIBA Intermediate standard. Surveyors and quantity surveyors are bound to be in short supply (the latter are always rare in developing countries) and it may be necessary to make expanded scholarship arrangements to prevent a serious bottleneck arising here as the development plan proceeds.

Commercial. The 1963 survey lists 821 accountants, auditors, company secretaries and bank officers in Category I and 1,786 book-keepers in Category II. These figures, however, do not cover a quarter of the senior commercial and industrial posts, nor a tenth of the Category II posts, which are covered in the over-all survey. The Rural and Industrial Development Agency College in Kuala Lumpur has residential accommodation for 50 girls and about 120 men and had an enrolment of 154 in 1962, evenly divided between courses in accountancy, secretaryship, 'general business' and stenography; the Technical College does not cover commercial subjects. In fact, most young Malayans learn their commercial skills on the job, sometimes under a good company training scheme, sometimes (more often) haphazardly. It is important that government should not saddle itself with the responsibility for complete commercial training-stenography, for example, can well be undertaken by private enterprise—but also that it should aid industry and commerce in their training programmes. The RIDA College is too constricted in site to expand largely; but there is surely room in Kuala Lumpur at least for a thriving commercial college, running a small group of full-time courses in certain definite skills—accountancy is one—and a very large programme of evening and day-release courses. It is from this area of evening-class work that most managers and executives are going to come.

Management. Managers are mainly produced by promotion from the ranks: but much can be done to help them enter the more senior ranks. The establishment in 1962 of a National Productivity Centre, with ILO assistance, in Petaling Japa should be immensely valuable in supervisory and management training. It is already running courses for senior and middle management in production, marketing, management accounting, etc., and for the supervisory level. There are proposals for courses for trade unionists, Malay contractors and many other groups. The centre has all the signs of energy and of acceptance by industry and commerce, and should fulfil a vital training role. Expansion of these activities would at present be much more valuable than any attempt to create a university department of commerce or business administration.

Artisan training. It remains to say that good artisan training is as important as the training of technicians; many technicians are, in fact, improved and promoted artisans. There will be an abundance of manpower with a background of education at least to form 3 and later to form 5. While all developing countries, owing to the small number of large employers, have had to create government trade schools, they are seldom satisfactory. Training centres associated with industrial estates (Johore, Kuala Lumpur,

Ipoh, Butterworth, with close relations with local employers) would probably meet the need, but very great care will have to be taken in training instructors.

Health Services

Statistics of government health staff in 1963 are: 451 doctors, 111 dentists, 21,747 hospital beds, 2,221 nurses, 122 dental nurses, 1,323 assistant nurses, 1,038 hospital assistants, 1,153 midwives, 269 health inspectors.

The fuller figures of the Medical Department for 1959 give a better picture of the detail of the public and private service.

TABLE 5.7

Doctors in the Public and Private Health Services

Service	*European*	*Indian*	*Malay*	*Chinese*	*Other*	*Total*
Government	118	229	29	84	11	471
Private	135	145	20	236	20	556
Total	253	374	49	320	31	1,027

At 1959, therefore, there was roughly one doctor to 7,000 population. Total dentists were 133, with 473 dental assistants. In addition to the nursing and other staff quoted above, there were 745 other medical staff at technician level, including radiographers, pharmacists, dispensers, anti-malaria inspectors, etc.

So many students are already launched on a course that initially the additional qualification for teaching may have to be given in a fourth, post-graduate, year. It may also be possible to start a three-year (B.Ed. or B.A.Ed. or B.Sc.Ed.) course to multiply numbers in the education stream. The vital qualification for a senior secondary teacher is a wide general knowledge of his subject and a lively interest in it.

The minor techniques of teaching can be quickly learned and are often over-emphasized by education departments.

It is therefore, recommended that the university review its plans for the production of teachers will urgency and determination. Science teachers must be borrowed from abroad for long enough—the more reason to see that some of the small output are encouraged to teach now. There should be enough arts students, even when the needs of the central administration are met, to man the secondary-school arts streams. It is easier to borrow even economists and statisticians than to borrow good teachers who can give continuity and standards to the senior secondary system upon which the whole manpower-policy of Malaysia depends.

GENERAL HIGH-LEVEL MANPOWER PROJECTIONS

The 1963 Survey of 'High-Level' Manpower carried out in the Federation showed stock in 1963 and estimates of requirements to 1971. It is clear that the 1971 estimates were possible to make in terms of real anticipated requirements in the absence of a plan and owing to the general impossibility of foreseeing economic conditions eight years ahead (by which time employers not yet in Malaya will be established and requiring staff). The provisional results of the survey were as follows:

A. KEY OCCUPATIONS

	Category I	*Category II*	*Total*
1963	6,988	20,536	27,524
1966 (estimate'	10,203	25,850	36,053
B. OVER-ALL TOTALS			
1963	11,945	34,288	46,233

It is clear that the over-all totals in particular are too low. Medical and dental personnel were omitted, and for this an addition of 1,500 Category I and 5,000 Category II must be made. There are some other categories (e.g., armed forces) which would have to be added (400 Category I, 1,000 Category II?). The agricultural sector may well have been 'downgraded' some-what. The key occupation lists give only 378 Category I estate managers and 132 in Category II. The 1957 census gives, in the agricultural sector; 'estate owners, managers, assistant managers, etc.; 3,600; conductors, 2,608'. It is clearly absurd to suggest that in the whole of Malaya the sum total of those who own and manage agricultural estates amounts to only 510, including Category II personnel.

A rough analysis of the 1957 census by occupations suggested figures of 13,500 for Category I and 48,000 Category II. If this is projected forward by six years to 1963, assuming 25 per cent wastage over six years and a gross addition of only 35 per cent in six years for Category I, and 50 per cent in six years for Category II, the result would be as follows:

Category	*Stock 1957* (1)	*Wastage* (2)	*Growth* (25 %)(3)	*Stock 1963* (1-2+3)
I	13,500	3,375	4,725 (35%)	14,850
II	48,000	12,000	24,000 (50%)	60,000

It is clear that the Category I figures for 1963 should be around the level of 15,000, or possibly 16,000 if all groups are included and if a more generous classification of agricultural managers is assumed. There is, however, a wider gap in the Category II figures, partly accounted for by the omission of medical personnel, armed forces and possibly some others, partly by the agricultural classification, partly by the inevitable differences where classification is so inexact, particularly in the commercial field. I believe a figure of 60,000 is nearer the mark for jobs which should by now be filled from candidates with secondary education ana further training.

To reach a figure of target stocks by 1970, by purely numerical projection, assuming 25 per cent economic growth and 50 per cent Category I and 75 per cent Category II additions over seven years, the figures are as follows:

Category	*Stock 1963 (1)*	*Wastage (25%) (2)*	*Growth (3)*	*Stock 1970 (1-2+3)*	*Annual output required*
I	16,000	4,000	8,000 (50 %)	20,000	1,143
II	60,000	15,000	45,000 (75 %)	90,000	6,430

To test the reasonableness of these figures, it may be noted that the result is to add only 6,500 to the 1957 census Category I stock over the thirteen-year period since 1957 (52 per cent) and 42,000 to Category II stock (90 per cent). The total growth for Category I plus II is just under 80 per cent. If the same relationship growth in Categories I and II respectively were applied to a higher rate of economic growth (say 35 per cent over seven years), the numerical result would be roughly 23,400 Category I and 105,000 Category II, a total of 128,000; the annual outputs (average over seven years) would be respectively 1,600 and 9,000.

Totals of 110,000 Categories I and II or 128,000 Categories I and II would represent 1.1 per cent and 1.3 per cent of 1970 population respectively. The higher figure is a reasonable target, representing just over double the 1957 total; it would imply that in the 1970s an output of over 2,000 a year to maintain and increase Category I and about 12,000 a year for Category II would be needed.

Education Implications

It is clear enough that an output of trainable students of 12,000 per annum from form 5 should easily we possible in the 1970's. Ministry of Education estimates for enrollments in form 5 were (in 1963, assisted schools only): 1967, 20,900; 1972, 26,800; 1977, 39,900. This leaves ample room for, say, 50 per cent falling gradually to 40 per cent to fail the School Certificate examination (a considerable improvement) and 25 per cent of passes to enter form 6(1), leaving nearly 8,000 School Certificate holders in 1967, 12,000 in 1972 and 18,000 in 1977 available for on-training.

Recruitment to Category I, if it is assumed to be made up as to 80 per cent of college graduates (university or professional technical college courses) is far more difficult. Even for a very moderate growth in the period 1963-70 an average output of about 1,000 per annum would be needed. This is certainly not in sight at present from the University and Technical College put together. The university has an expected output of 800 by as late as 1968. It is clear that every possible effort must be made to increase university entry in the immediate future. It is stimulated that 2,250 students will be enrolled in form 6(2) by 1967 and this would create pressure for a university entry of well over 1,500 in 1968, rising to 2,000 by 1970 and to nearly 3,000 by 1972. The sequence can be set out as follows:

	Form 5	*School Certificate passes*	*On-training*	*To form 6(1)*	*University entry*
1965 1966	16,000	8,000	5,750	2,250	1,500
1967	20,900	10,500	7,875	2,625	1,800
1968 1969	21,500	11,000	8,250	2,750	2,000
1970 1971	24,000	14,000	10,500	3,500	2,750
1972 1973-1974	26,800	16,000	12,000	4,000	3,000 plus

It is clear from these figures than an extremely rapid acceleration in university entry would be necessary to achieve the 1970-75 targets. A new university college with an entry of 300 students in 1967 and a second new colleges in about 1971-72 would give figures of:

Entry 1967 Kuala Lumpur 1,200 + 1 new college 300 = 1,500

Entry 1970 Kuala Lumpur 1,500 + 1 new college 500 = 2,000

Entry 1972 Kuala Lumpur 1,800 + 2 new colleges 900 = 2,700

The figures would imply a total university population of about 6,250 (3.5 years' entry) in 1970 including the 1970 entry, and of about 8,000 in 1972 and of 10,000 in 1975, with an output of graduates rising from 1,250 in 1970 to 2,500 in 1975 and 3,000 later in the decade. The 1975 population would be distributed between Kuala Lumpur (6,500), first new college (2,000) and second new college (1,500).

These figures represent only a 'model' of what would be necessary to achieve the output figure at School Certificate and university degree level required by the suggested rate of manpower growth. To achieve such a target involves overcoming many difficulties in the educational system, in particular the problems of language, the recruitment and training of Malay-stream teachers and of graduate science teachers in secondary schools. It involves a considerable improvement in School Certificate performance. It involves great expansion of post-secondary training facilities. It involves heavy financial outlay. But the greatest difficulty of all will be the recruitment of secondary and university teaching staff adequate for the student populations envisaged. Staff in such numbers cannot be found within Malaysia at present. It follows that they are likely to be English-speaking. To insist on Malay as the only university language of instruction would be to abandon such a programme.

Whether this programme is desirable or necessary is for the Government to judge. It is certain that decisions already taken to enlarge secondary education will be followed by enormous pressure for more university places; and that a university population of 10,000 in the early 1970s is a relatively modest programme in terms of Malaya's estimated population of 10 million by then—it is just one-tenth of 1 per cent—and of the maintained obligation to assist Sabah and Sarawak.

Conclusion

There are three strategic areas in which Malayan manpower policy requires adjustment.

First, a greater concentration on food production and diversification of economic crops, involving a large increase in field and research staff.

Second, primary and secondary education have been expanded to ratios which have outrun university provision. It is suggested that one new university college is needed by 1967 and a second by 1971-72.

Third, and of highest priority, existing and planned production of graduate secondary teachers is far below requirements; a clear and determined decision is needed to guide students into teaching and to reward them adequately, even at the expense of output in certain subjects which have a value in themselves and will come into their own when—and only when—the foundations of manpower production have been well laid in the secondary schools.

6

Education in Latin America

There is doubt in the minds of many people whether a cultural unit called Latin America truly exists. There is a vast difference between Brazil and E1 Salvador; between Mexico and Argentina; and between Cuba and the Dominican Republic. These differences are in size, political structure, composition of the population, degrees of economic and social development, natural environment, and even in historical background. How can one describe, much less establish a policy or strategy for all of the American Republics? Yet those countries to the south of us which we call Latin America do share a body of cultural heritage. This common heritage derives from their common Iberian background, from the fact that they were colonies of Spain and Portugal, and that since independence they have been in an economic colonial status vis-a-vis Europe and the United States. Furthermore, in varying degrees they share some common economic and social problems, not only among themselves, but with other less developed countries of the world. Such problems are a rapidly expanding population, an illiterate peasantry, exploding cities, an economic dependency upon the export of raw materials such as Chilean copper and Brazilian coffee, political instability, the maldistribution of land, the pains of nascent industrialization, the frustration of a growing middle class, the ills of inflation, and the weight of debt on borrowed capital.

The systems of higher education in these Latin American countries reflect their common Iberian heritage, their colonial past, and the current social and economic problems which have been briefly listed above. But it must be said each country has its own system of education, its own educational problems, and its own educational history. At the beginning of this century, Argentina was already a predominantly literate society while just to the north Brazil was predominantly illiterate. Peru has had the problem of educating people who speak an indigenous language (Quecha) while in Chile only a hundred thousand people or so did not speak Spanish. In any case, in this paper I shall discuss some problems of Latin America that seem to be common to much of the region, if not to other countries of the modern world.

First, it must be said that in the nineteenth century and during the first decades of this century, all Latin American countries were elitist oriented. Out of the colonial past they had inherited a rigid class structure that divided their societies into a small aristocracy and into a mass of poor and illiterate peons and urban workers. Education was for the elite, and it was aimed at forming cultured humanistic gentlemen. The ideal man toward which education was oriented was described by Jose Enrique Rodo in his famous essay *Ariel* published in 1900. He dedicated his essays to the "Youth of America", and in it, he pleaded with the youth of Latin America not to imitate the crass materialistic Yankee to the north whom he compared to Caliban, the animalistic slave of Prospero in Shakespeare's *The Tempest*. He urged that education be aimed at creating a society of Ariels, similar to the sensitive, spiritual, humanistic woodsprite liberated from bondage by Prospero in this same play. Arielismo, as it is called, became the dominant ideology in Latin American higher education. Thus, philosophy, the arts, literature, and humanistic subjects overshadowed science, technology, and the applied sciences. Latin American higher education still suffers from Arielismo, but the scene is changing rapidly in the second half of the twentieth century.

Early Reforms

As early as 1918, Latin American university students found their educational systems out of keeping with the world of their time, although most of them seemed to accept the ideal of Arielismo. In that year in the provincial Argentine University of Corrdoba, the students went on indefinite strike, occupied administrative offices, and presented a series of demands for university reform. They demanded student participation along with professors and alumni in university government. They asked that university authorities such as the *rector* (i.e., the president or chancellor) be elected for a specific term. They asked for freedom from obligatory attendance at classes and free tuition. They demanded that the curriculum be revised and be related to national problems and issues. And they demanded that the university be "autonomous", that, is free from political and administrative interference from the Government.

The Cordoba movement or the Cardoba Reform spread rapidly throughout Latin America, although a large number of countries remained unconvinced or, as in Brazil, did not as yet have universities to reform. But in many Latin American universities, particularly the large national universities. Students have been admitted to the governing bodies, participated in electing deans and rectors. Throughout Latin America university autonomy became almost a sacred concept which even the most powerful of dictators or military governments have hesitated to break. One cannot say that the university curriculum was drastically overhauled; for, in fact, these same rebellious students of the 1920s were still elitists. But, to us in the United States, this university reform, begun as long ago as 1918 in Latin America, sounds strangely modern. The demands of the students seem very much like those coming from our students in the late 1960s. At Columbia University, it was only after the students' strike of 1968 that a University Senate was formed in 1969 with elected student senators and that students were allowed to participate in crucial university committees. We have not come to the point that we allow faculty and students to elect our university presidents, but in many institutions they are demanding that they be consulted on such appointments. At least one president of a great North American university has suggested that the office of president be held for a term of seven years. Could it be that we in the United States are so far behind Latin America in university reform?

It must be said that the Latin American University reform did not solve many educational problems. It probably created more administrative problems than it solved. But most certainly Latin American university students have had until recently a greater voice in educational policies and in national affairs than in the United States. In fact, it used to be said that one should watch the politics of university students to plot the direction of political developments of any Latin American country. The university reform did provide students with considerable political power (this is less the case today); but the reform was less profound educationally. It did not really modify the elitist structure of higher education nor the essential classical and humanistic character of the curriculum. On the whole. Latin American universities continued to be out of keeping with the needs of their respective nations. To understand why this is so, one must look at the whole system of education and the societies they are supposed to serve, not just at the institutions of higher education.

The Educational Systems and Social Needs

Latin American educational systems are full of paradoxes and dilemmas. On the one hand, there are universities older than any in the United Statess such as the University of San Marcos in Lima, Peru. On the other hand, there are universities founded in the last few years, so new that they are housed in temporary buildings and without regular faculty. There are faculties and institutes of higher education of great distinction such as the Technological Institute in Monterrey in Mexico, the Biological Institute of Sao Paulo in Brazil, the Venezuelan Scientific Institute and others too numerous to mention. There are also faculties of higher education without adequate facilities and manned by ill-trained and part-time teachers. Most Latin American countries have an enormous range of schools and faculties of higher education covering almost every known speciality in the arts and sciences, applied sciences, and the professions. Yet most Latin American countries still do not have sufficient facilities nor personnel in higher education to train the people necessary for their needs in social and economic development.

With a total population of over 250 million people in all of Latin America, there are less than 750,000 men and women enrolled in schools and faculties of higher education. With a population of more than 90 million people, Brazil claims just over 250,000 university students, which is less than those in the metropolitan area of New York City. The fact is that higher education in Latin America is still for an elite group, although it now recruits from a much larger social spectrum than before. This apparent underdevelopment of higher education is a reflection of the whole system of education and not just the lack of funds nor even the motivation of people to seek advanced training.

All Latin American countries theoretically provide free and compulsory primary education. But despite enormous efforts and considerable expenditure of funds, it is estimated that as many as 15 million children of primary school age do not attend school. Either schools are too distant from their homes; their parents need their labour; or the schools do not have room for them. Furthermore, it is estimated that nine out of ten children who begin primary school drop out before finishing the course. Yet, secondary schools have expanded vertigiously throughout Latin America in the last two or three decades. This is due primarily to the rapid growth of a small town and urban middle class who want education for their children and are able to see them through the primary years. In Brazil, for example, a country that was notably lacking in secondary schools a generation ago, there has been an explosion of secondary education. In 1946, Brazil had but 417 schools of secondary education with but 66,420 students. By 1967, there were 20 times that number of secondary schools and more than 2,800,000 students. More than half of these schools were private, charging tuition, thus eliminating many students for economic reasons.

These secondary schools private an admirably planned curriculum, modeled to a large extent upon the French Iycee system which stresses classical and scholastic subjects, but few of them have the faculty and the facilities to actually carry out what they promise. Again the dropout rate is enormous, perhaps even greater than for elementary schools. Throughout most of Latin America, as in Brazil, only a tiny fraction of students actually complete secondary education—perhaps only 1 out of 100 of the youths was began primary school. There are, then, very few students who qualify for higher education. The educational system from the beginning acts as a funnel or filter weeding out those who might go on to university.

Yet Latin American universities are more overcrowded than those in the United States despite the obstacles in primary and secondary education which allow but few to reach higher education. Latin American countries are being forced to adopt a mass-type system of higher education. The tremendous rate of population growth, the expansion of secondary education, and the need for trained personnel in all fields of endeavour have resulted in a rapid expansion of the university population. There are more young people knocking at the doors for admission to schools and faculties of higher education than can be handled with present facilities and professorial personnel.

There are two "solutions," neither of them satisfactory, which the Latin American University systems have adopted. First, there is the solution of selective admissions. A certain number of openings are made available in each faculty, calculated upon the availability of space and faculty. Candidates are admitted on the basis of secondary school records and examinations. Brazil is a good example of a country that has adopted the selective admissions policy. Strict admissions examinations are given for each faculty. A student must often take a special preparatory course for the examinations which are private and relatively expensive. An examination for admissions for one faculty of engineering, for example, is not valid for another for there is no national system of admission examinations. The number of failures is high especially for the prestigious schools of medicine, engineering and law; often four out of five candidates are failed. Sometimes, although there may be 300-400 openings, the faculty decides that only 200-300 have done well enough to pass, thus leaving unfilled places even in well-equipped universities. On the other hand, certain schools and faculties are undersubscribed; that is, there are not enough candidates in the examinations to fill their first-year classes. Nursing, veterinary medicine, agronomy, and other professions of less prestige sometimes cannot fill their quota of students, while in medicine, engineering, law, and other prestige professional schools a student might take admission examinations several times in an attempt to be admitted.

The other so-called solution is open admission, which is not being revived in some universities in the United States. By this method any student with a secondary education and the proper courses has the right to enter university. Some countries, such as Argentina and Mexico, have adopted a modified form of open admission. This has brought about a flooding of universities with the inevitable result that many badly prepared students are allowed to enter. It creates a situation where it is easy to get in but hard to get out; in other words, only a small portion of those who enter the university actually graduate. Students fail and repeat courses, and they may take many years to complete all of the examinations leading to a degree. Students are enrolled but do not (many cannot) attend classes. The University of Buenos Aires in recent years had a total enrollment of more than 80,000 students, and the National University of Mexico had more than 90,000. Neither university could probably seat all of its students if they, by chance, came to class on the same day. Under such circumstances, university education becomes as impersonal and automatic as in many large states universities of the United States and of Europe.

Whatever the admissions policy, the Latin American student faces a rigid university curriculum. There are few elective courses, even in faculties of arts and sciences or philosophy and letters which are apt to be the more flexible. The most sought after faculties continue to be law, medicine, and engineering as they were in Rodo's era in 1900, despite a recent effort to emphasize public administration, economics, teacher training, and the applied sciences. In general, Latin American higher education is much more diverse than before, offering a large range of special fields; but it is almost as much out of tune with national priorities as it was before the Cordoba Reform movement. It still produces lawyers who will never practice law and physicians who balk at working in small towns or rural zones but who set up practice in the large cities where the competition in medicine is fierce. Latin American societies do not as yet offer a sufficient market for some of their most highly trained technicians and scientists who often seek employment abroad for economic and sometimes political reasons. Despite the excellent research institutes and the multiplication of faculties, there are not enough positions for natural and physical scientists nor for many people in the special fields of applied science in industry.

Educational Planning and Financing

The problems of Latin American higher education are not being solved for lack of planning, nor often for the lack of funds. Latin American governments have been spending an increasing amount each year on higher education in relation to their national budgets. In fact, there sometimes seems to be a veritable flood of university reform plans in Latin America. Latin American university administrators are fully aware of new trends in higher education. As one educator put it, almost every letter from abroad (i.e., the United States and Europe) brings new solutions for our educational problems. There are co-operative programs between Latin American and North American universities such as that between the School of Agronomy in Minas Gerais (Brazil) and Purdue University (United States). North American and European foundations have made financial grants to improve Latin American institutions of higher learning and research, often with considerable success. Furthermore, the structure for national planning is present in most Latin American countries. Brazil has a Board of Higher Education (Conselho Federal de Educacao), a National Science Foundation (Conselho Nacional de Pesquizas) and CAPES (Co-ordenacao do Aperfeicoamento de Pessoal de

Nivel Superior), which is dedicated to the improvement of university personnel and curriculum. Chile has a National Council of University Rectors who meet to establish national plans. And there are international organizations such as the Regional Inter-University Council which brings together the "national" universities of Argentina, Chile, Peru and Uruguay and the Supreme University Council of Central America which aims at co-operative planning and activities. And CHEAR (Council on Higher Education in the Americas) has for 15 years provided informal meetings of university officials from both North and South America and has carried out several important studies of American university systems. Latin American institutions of higher education do not live in isolation, and if they are sometimes called archaic it is not for lack of knowledge of higher education in other parts of the world.

Furthermore, it would seem that it might not be difficult to bring about changes in Latin American universities. Most of them are public, and the largest are supported by the national governments. A few public universities are supported by states, such as the University of Sao Paulo in Brazil; and some are private, that is, founded and supported by non-governmental organizations. Most of these private universities are Catholic, but a few are secular such as the University of the Andes in Bogota. But even such private universities receive considerable direct and indirect support from public funds. Furthermore, Latin American governments have control over private institutions through regulations concerning curriculum, registration of diplomas, and other mechanisms. There tends to be greater central control over higher education throughout Latin America than in the United States. This would seem to provide the structure for national planning and development.

Obstacles to Change

Resistance to change, however, seems to derive not from lack of knowledge nor from the lack of a national planning body but from the internal structure of the universities themselves. One of the most astute and profound university administrators in Latin America once said that he had no difficulty in establishing a rational plan for the "new Latin American university" but asked, "how can I change the professors and the student?" He might have added: how can I change the entrenched internal structure of the Latin American university? Most Latin American universities are not universities in the sense of unified corporate organizations. Most of them grew out of independent faculties and technical schools taking the form more of a federation than a single large unit. Most universities do not have a campus in the same sense that most universities in the United States do, although there is a trend to build "university cities" in an attempt to provide a central locale. Most Latin American universities do not have a central library. Instead each faculty, sometimes each "chair" or department such as sociology or physics, has its separate library. University-wide affairs often are limited to a few solemn acts carried out collectively, and sometimes there may be a unified approach in dealing with the government concerning funds or university autonomy. Generally, each faculty guards its independence as far as possible—in curriculum, admission of students, rules for students, recruitment of faculty, and other institutional functions. There is often a duplication of facilities, courses and staff. For example, the same level course in, say, mathematics or physics, may be taught in several faculties of the same university. This fragmentation and independence of faculties is, of course, a heritage from Europe, but as a system it is not feasible economically or intellectually for countries with an urgent need to expand higher education. Nor does it seem efficient even for richer nations such as the United States or France.

Another focus of resistance to change in Latin American systems of higher education is the professors. Most, but not all, Latin American universities have by now modified or abandoned the traditional system of the "Catedra" (The Chair), by which there was one tenured professor in each field—a "Catedratico" of physics, of sociology, of European history and the like. In that system, all other teachers in the same field were but lecturers and subordinates. There was no position for a rising young scholar until the returned professor retired or died. This tended to fragment the university even more, for in each faculty there were generally little "kingdoms" presided over by the "Catedratico." Most universities, forced by increasing numbers of students and pressure from younger faculty, now have multiple chairs in one field of study and have created careers for teachers in lower ranks. But in many professional schools and in some more traditional universities the concept of the single "owner of the chair" still prevails. Such entrenched individuals are hardly anxious for change in the system.

It is well known that most Latin American professors give only part-time to the university. Hardly any place are they paid well enough to live from their positions at the university without other sources of income. It has been said that "a professorship is an honour, not an occupation." Thus, a large percentage of Latin American teachers augment by necessity their incomes from business, journalism, industry, and other occupations; many of them teach in several faculties. One professor in Brazil, for example, taught sociology for a time in three separate faculties. With such a system, there is little time to spend with students out of class, and any research activities are generally done outside the university setting, often to augment income.

In recent years, there has been a trend throughout Latin America toward the "full-time" university professor.

Of course, the full-time professor must be paid a better salary. One way of achieving full-time and of attempting to break the pattern of university fragmentation is the creation of university-wide institutes, such as an Institute of Physics and an Institute of Economics. In theory, the research and the teaching of a particular subject would be lodged in the institute, and the faculty of an institute would be devoted full-time to teaching and research. In several instances such institutes have become outstanding research and teaching organizations, but too often the faculties have tended to hold on to teaching and the institutes have become devoted to research and sometimes teaching on a very advanced level. Generally, it would seem that the central institute has been a solution more for the faculty than for the student; institutes create the equivalent of another position and provide better facilities for research. They do also provide a basis for the training of advanced students through participation in research. But one of the great needs of Latin American education is still the formation of a corps of full-time professionals devoted to university activities.

Equally important is the creation of a student body free to devote themselves full-time to their studies. Latin American students do not resist change in the university system; in fact, if one interprets their demands correctly, they are eager for change. But under the present circumstances they could not really study under any system that demanded more of then time and energy. The majority of university students are part-time. Even more, many Latin American students hold full-time jobs and are able to attend classes only in the late afternoon and evening—or in hours stolen from their jobs. This is less true in medicine and other technical schools than in arts and science and philosophy and letters. In one study carried out in Buenos Aires some years ago, only 30 per cent of all students were supported by their families, while 52 per cent of the medical students had full family support. In this same study, it was found that 90 per cent of the university students lived at home with their parents, or in their own homes in the case of the few that were married. There are few scholarships available, and although tuition is free or relatively cheap at least in the public universities, families cannot afford to support their children as they seek higher degrees.

This does not mean that many Latin American university students derive from poverty-stricken families. Latin American universities now draw students predominantly from the middle class. Throughout Latin America the middle class is growing, especially in countries such as Argentina, Brazil, Chile, Venezuela, Colombia, Mexico, and others where economic development is rapid. Those in the new middle class are ambitious for their children. They do not want their children to work with their hands as some of them did. There is almost a cult of degrees in the new bureaucratic societies in which this new middle class lives; degrees are the passage necessary for positions. And middle-class parents want their sons and daughters to be physicians, engineers, lawyers, school teachers, and the like. They urge their children to enter university, but their incomes are generally not sufficient to support them during the extra years of study.

Student Activism

Most major Latin American universities are urban; most Latin American students live at home. The students, then, reflect the values of their urban middle-class parents. There is a long-standing stereotype that the Latin American student is a wild-eyed radical, urged on by agitators who may be just "professional" students, and uninterested in studying. Latin American universities to have their quota of radicals and agitators; and traditionally student politics have been more heated that in the United States because students have had a greater voice in internal university affairs and even in national politics. But all serious studies of Latin American students indicate that they are far from wild-eyed radicals; most of them are fully aware of the privileged position they have by virtue of reaching the university. One seasoned observer of the Latin American universities has this to say: "Probably the majority of students in state universities are more secular than not, more nationalist than not, more middle class than not, more centre and left-centre than not, and more worried about individual fortune than the fate of the state". "Student strikes have been a weapon more often used by students in Latin America than in the United States, but often such strikes have been aimed against serious invasions of academic freedom or student rights by autocratic governments.

One of the reasons why the outsider sees Latin American students as radicals is their fundamental and deep-seated nationalism. Latin American nationalism is based upon a pride of their own nations, but like nationalism everywhere it has it negative aspects. It was fostered by the anti-Americanism of the nineteenth century which Arielismo helped perpetuate and was reinforced by mistakes in U.S. policy toward Latin America—such as intervention in Guatemala, the Dominican Republic, and Cuba—and by the growth of American economic power and investments in their countries. Latin American students thus tend to blame the United States for many of the ills of their countries. To be blunt, it is the impression of many people who have worked with Latin American students that they distrust, even rabidly dislike, the United States for what it represents today in the international scene. But this anti-Americanism should not be confused with political radicalism, not with a dislike of the North American people and their achievements.

The situation of many Latin American universities is today truly disheartening to say the least. In several countries both students and faculty are faced with military regimes which have imposed strict limitations on academic freedom and research. In other countries with relatively democratic governments, the universities are apt to be viewed as foci of opposition to be controlled for the benefit of tranquillity and economic development. Hardly a day goes by without news of a university protest, demonstration, or strike. Few Latin American universities go through a full academic year without interruptions. Latin American professors and research scientists are attracted to Europe and to the United States, not only for larger salaries, but for the right to teach freely and to carry on their research without political intervention. Not only are Latin American universities under pressure from their governments, but it must be said that most of them operate by an archaic system which is based upon social values, methods, and facilities which are out of date with the modern world. If this situation continues, one wonders how the Latin American countries will be able to train a new generation of administrators, technicians, professionals, teachers, and all those leaders needed to man their increasingly complex societies.

Yet, all of these troubles of Latin American higher education are not unique in the modern world. In 1968 French university rebelled against the archaic university structure and the lack of facilities in their universities. In the United States we are now confronted with student dissatisfaction and student strikes. Our students are becoming more articulate and activist, especially in face of United States involvement in the war in Southeast Asia and the problems of the ghettos of the great cities. Students in the United States are asking questions about how and what we teach in our own universities, and they are questioning the structure of the North American university itself. North American students are beginning to sound like and act like Latin American students.

And, paradoxically, North American universities are becoming more similar to Latin American Universities. Students are more highly politicized and will soon be able to express themselves by vote (people over 18 years of age have been electors for many years in most Latin American countries). Students are now represented on university senates and even on boards of trustees. Open admission versus selective admission is being debated in the United States and one of our great public universities, the City University of New York, has adopted an open admission policy. As Latin American universities turn to mass education and as the universities of the United States begin to deal with more varied and less complacent types of students, there seems to be a convergence in the kinds of problems each system faces. As many Latin American universities attempt to "improve themselves," often on the pattern of the United States, it seems to many North American educators that we are becoming "Latinized" as our centres of higher education take on the complexion of these in Latin America.

In Latin America and in the United States, the future of higher education is one of the fundamental problems of today. As societies become more complex both socially and technologically, the body of knowledge which must be transmitted from one generation to another increases almost geometrically. We are faced with "new" problems not even envisaged a generation ago, and we can hardly imagine the problems that the next generation will be called upon to solve. How could a professor of my generation imagine the degree of pollution which this generation must suffer or the importance to the next generation of pollution control? How could one have predicted that in 1971. The City University of New York would have an enrollment of over 150,00 students? How could one imagine that the city of Sao Paulo in Brazil would have over 6 million people? How can one imagine that same city 20 years hence may have 20 to 30 million people? How can this generation of students imagine what their lives and their societies will be like in the year 2000? One thing is certain, higher education will and must change throughout the world. We can no longer hang onto the hoary traditions of the past. This is as true for Latin America as it is for the United States and Europe. University reform is much more crucial today than it was in the time of

7

Education in Thailand

General

The education and manpower needs of Thailand have been intensive studied in the last year, and it is necessary for this report to go through the basic data in detail. What follows therefore mainly devoted to certain comments on key issues. If I have interpreted the reports correctly, there has been a fundamental confusion between what manpower the economy as such needs for continued progress and what shape the educational system of Thailand is likely to take, or should take, regarded simply as an educational, social and political problem. After brief comments on the economy and the bare facts of educational enrolments and outputs, a section of this report will deal with this central issue: the fifth section deals with certain special sectors, in an attempt to indicate minimum requirements of high-level manpower to sustain economic growth and reasonable education expansion.

Both in education and in economic atmosphere Thailand could be regarded as half-way house between Malaya and the Philippines. Education has not mushroomed as in the Philippines, but at University level has overrun the tight quality-control and shortage of numbers of Malaya. The economy, welcoming both internal and foreign private enterprise, is less highly administered than in Malaya, perhaps a little more socialize, than the *laissez-faire* philosophy of business in Manila. In consequence, the planner is faced in Thailand with a great deal of individualism socially, educationally and economically, which produdes any rigidit, in planning; but none of less Government has a considerable planning mechanism for giving direction and balance to development.

The Economy

From various projections of population growth, this study is using that adopted by the Unesco Advisory Team (population in thousands); 1960, 26,990; 1965, 31,777; 1970, 37,537; 1975, 44,579; 1980, 53.291. This assumes rates of population growth rising from 3.3 per cent in 1960-65 to 3.6 per cent in 1975-80. Population in 1962 is assumed to be 28.8 million.

Gross national product has been rising lately at between 6 and 7 per cent, giving a *per capita* income of approximately £37 in 1962.

The economy is primarily agricultural, with about 82 per cent of those economically active in agricultural pursuits (commerce 5.6 per cent; services 4 per cent; manufacturing, 3.4 per cent; remainder 4.6 per cent—1960 population census). Agriculture, however, produces only 36 per cent of GNP. This percentage has fallen from 50 per cent in 1951, indicating a large rise in the non-agricultural sector. Employment in manufacturing was 470,000 in 1960, estimated to grow to 658,000 in 1966: but this includes cottage industry, etc. Employment by firms employing ten or more probably did not exceed 100,000-120,000 in 1962. No accurate figures are available. Major exports are, in order of importance (1962 value in million baht): rice, 3,301; rubber, 2,111; tin, 690; jute and kenaf, 589; maize, 502; tapioca products, 423; teak, 170; custor seeds, 124; cattle, 103; kapok, 102; total 8,115. The total of these ten exports represents 84.5 per cent of all exports; rice and rubber alone represent 56.3 per cent of the total. The balance of trad has recently been adverse (consistently since 1952), reaching an adverse total of 1,974 million baht in 1962 (nearly £34 million). This deficit has been mainly due to heavy imports of machinery, fuel, chemicals and manufactured goods. The balance has been met partly by foreign investment and partly by international aid on a large scale.

The remarkable rise in national income is in part due to additional agricultural production (but this is estimated as only 58 per cent for 1951-62); partly by heavy investment in the development of Bangkok and huge foreign aid spent there; partly to quite rapidly increasing industrialization. Industry in Thailand has the makings of a'heavy' sector—a large iron foundry, a large unit galvanizing and corrugating iron sheet, a sheet-rolling and aluminium-rolling mill, some non-ferrous metal work, in oil refinery and a chemical fertilizer plant. There is to be tyre factory, large cement mills, and a growing amount of truck and car assembly. Gunny-bags, pharmaceuticals, textiles, plywood, minor engineering, sugar, rice and sawmills may be mentioned among a large number of secondary and processing industries. The Board of Investment lists 141 certificates issued for new firms, and another 125 approved or under consideration (October 1963) Capital involved for the 141 (firms to whom certificates were issued was 2,029 million baht (£34 million). Power supply will be more than adequate—though it is at present too expensive—and a considerable programme of road improvement is planned and financed but proceeding slowly. Bangkok particularly has been a boom town for some years, attracting alike tourists, foreign missions and agencies of all kinds, and foreign investors. It is, however, significant that after the 3 million population of the Bangkok-Thonburi complex the next largest town in Thailand is Chiengmai, with a population of 56,000.

In the agricultural sector progress is less encouraging. Rice yields, though ahead of Burma or the Philippines, are still far behind the leading Asian produces (about 215 kg. per rai in 1962 against 709 in Japan (1957) or 467 in Taiwan (1957). There has been considerable diversification recently, and in particular the prospects for cotton in the driver areas seem extremely hopeful. Schemes for irrigation and flood control, the use of fertilizer, and the opeing of better communication should all increase agricultural potential. But the real revolution in agricultural productivity is till far ahead in the future.

In summary the Thailand economy rests first upon a huge and quite comfortable agricultural population, which has not yet been stirred to more than moderate efforts, so that a population increase of 3.5 per cent will catch up with production and eat into export earnings unless there is a considerable rise in productivity. Secondly, it rests upon a fast growing industrial sector which is, however, very small in relation to total population and labour force. Thirdly, upon a commercial and construction boom based on Bangkok with its attractions for foreign spending and investment.

The Educational System

The educational system was originally directed into a four-year primary courses (Paratom I-IV) and an eight-year secondary courses (Matayom 1-8) broken by Matayom 3 which was the end of the junior secondary stage, and at Mayom 6, before the last two years of pre-university work. It is now a seven-year primary courses (Pratom 1-7) followed by a five-year secondary courses (Matayon Suksa 1-5), broken at MS 3 (the old Matayom 6). MS 4 and 5 are the two pre-university years.

Primary, 1961 (1962)

Total I-IV	*I*	*IV*	*Total V-VII*	*V*	*VII*	*Total I-VII*
3,716,969	1,322,855	657,313	375,953	137,054	112,714	4,092,922
(3,721,308)			(364,826)			(4,086,134).

It is estimated that from 1,000 children in standard 1,696 reach Standard VI and 136 reach Standard VII. Private schools represent about 10 per cent of the enrolment in standards I-IV, almost 50 per cent in V-VII.

General Secondary, 1961 (1962)

MS 1-3	*Ms 1*	*MS 3*	*MS 4-5*	*MS 4*	*MS 5*	*Total MS 1-5*
236,244	93,790	66,496	34,,512	22.091	12,421	270,756
(251,236)	—	—	(36.094)	—	—	(287,330).

It is estimated that out of 1,000 children entering primary Standard I, only 121 enter MS 1; 18 reach MS 3 and 31 enter MS 5. Private schools represent 43.5 per cent of MS 1-3 and 55.5 per cent of MS 4 and 5. It is interesting that over 70 per cent of secondary enrolment is the science streams.

Vocational Education, 1961

'Short time'	*Junior Vocational*	*Senior vocational*	*High vocational*	*Technical*
1923	666	16,880	29,327	4,891
			Graduates, 1961	
		5,949	8,796	1,673

'Senior vocational' corresponds to MS 1-3, 'higher educational' to MS 4-5 with one additional year (i.e., to grade 13). Technical institutes run to grades 14, 15 and sometimes 16, corresponding to three or four years of university work. There is considerable evidence that senior vocational schools are becoming increasingly unpopular, and applications are falling. There is substantial unemployment among graduates from these funds. There remain strong competition forestry into higher vocational and technical courses.

University Education

The total enrolment in universities in 1961 was approximately 40,900 and in 1962,42,100. But these figures include a very large number of part-time of even nominal enrolments at Thammasart. These Thammasart enrolments were regarded as the equivalent of 2,500 full-time enrolments by the Unesco mission. In fact, about 7,000 students were regularly attending lectures at Thammasart in 1963, and it would possibly be preferable to allow 5,000 students, bringing the total enrolled in all university education to 16,500 or thereabouts: Chulalongkorn, 6,223; Thammasart, 5,000; Kasetsart, 2,101; Medical, 2,966; Silpakorn, 350; total 16,640.

Table 10 shows the division by subjects studies and graduations (42,000 students, i.e., including Thammasart at full nominal strength) in 1962.

TABLE 8.1

University Education: Enrollments and Graduations, 1962

Subject	*Enrollment*		*Degree*	*Diploma*
Natural science, engineering	3017		401	254
Humanities, arts	33,153	(7.11)	1,651	171
Medicine and nursing	3,150		392	177
Agriculture	2,101		241	333
Education	682		214	18
Total	42,104	(16,640)	2,899	953

The new university in Chiengmai has had a Medical School from which the first graduates will emerge in 1964. Other faculties open in 1964. The University of Khonkaen (or the Institute of Technology) will admit students in 196-65.

In 1963 about 20,000 students applied for 5,000 places in Thai universities. There were only about 12,000 enrolled in MS 5, so that many applicants must have come from earlier years. Many applicants have not passed the entry examination, and many of these gain admission—in fact 700 out of 933 admissions to Thammasart in 1963 had failed the entry examination, and this applies to other universities, although in unknown proportions. Usually about 60 per cent has the final MS 5 examination, so that every year there are 7,000 (rising to 8,000) new applicants for about 5,000 (rising to 6,000) places, apart from those who make a second attempt. It may be that well under half actually pass the university entry tests.

Education and Manpower Demands

In this section an attempt is made to distinguish between education demands—that is, a programme which will give some satisfaction to the popular demand for education and keep some gradual rise in educational attainment of the population as a whole; and economic manpower demands that is, the requirement for particular types of education and training necessary to maintain economic progress. This distinction cannot be precise and rigid: quite clearly, some economic effect is produced by an output of far more graduates than appear to be necessary for the economy. But at some point financial considerations have to be taken into account (since the investment in education, whether private or public, is at the expense of some other investment): further, social expectations and disappointments can be important, if the attainment of a certain educational level does not reward the graduate with employment of the type which he thereby expects. The distinction is thereby useful in analysis.

Thailand, by 1960, had already accumulated a large stock of manpower with some higher education. The census of 1960 shows a total stock of 95,137 with some college education, and 618,997 with some secondary (MS 1-5). This amounts to 2.6 percent of total population, a percentage far higher than any probable number of Category I and II posts. However, a high proportion off these were not economically active: the labour force, 15 years and over, in 1960, included 56,290 with college attainment (of whom nearly 17,000 were women), and 400,000 MS 1-5 (including 92,000 women). Further, it includes a higher proportion of 'own account' workers and 'others' compared to the number of employees:

	Employers, government and private employees	'Own account' or 'Others'	Total
College attainment	38,024	18,266	56,290
MS 1-5	102,600	297,400	400,000

One further fact may be mentioned from the 'educational attainment' figures—only 27,000 of total population had four years of college or more.

While among college graduates quite a large number of posts would be held by 'own account' workers, neither employing nor employed (for example, doctors, lawyers, etc.), it seems less likely that the very large number of secondary graduates could have been a high-level occupations under these headings. Many were, no doubt, women doing part-time work, and many of the men must have been in fairly modest occupations.

We thus have a picture of a society in which higher education is much valued and sought after; in which quite large numbers of those who had been to college were not actively engaged in the economy; in which large numbers of women gained higher education, many of them no doubt to manage family business affairs; in which an unusually high proportion are described as 'own account' workers, including many with only a partial secondary education; in which government employment is highly valued and much over-supplied. It is a society of considerable private individual self-reliant effort to find a niche in affairs from which a living can be gained, though not necessarily a 'high-level' niche; and a society with a small 'modern sector' of fairly recent origin. It would be surprising if formal employment in high-level posts was very large. In fact, a rough analysis of census occupational data, as used elsewhere in its report, suggests a relatively low number of Categories I and II posts—roughly 30,000 in Category I and 70,000 in Category II. These figures are not so very far from the 38,000 university and 102,000 secondary graduates which include all employers and employees, recollecting that the 102,000 include those who only reached the first year of higher secondary education and would not normally be automatically included in Category II potential.

The ten-year projections from my Categories I and II figures, assuming 60 per cent economic growth, 120 per cent Category I and 180 per cent Category II growth over ten years, gives the following result:

Category	*Stock 1960*	*Ten-Year wastage (40%)*	*Ten-year growth (120 % I: 180 % II)*	*Required Ten-year requirement*	*output per annum*
I	30,000	12,000	36,000	48,000	4,800
II	70,000	28,000	126,000	154,000	15,400

If we now turn to the projections of outputs required made by the Thai USOM Task Force and by the Unesco Educational Investment Mission, we find that the annual average requirements for 1960-66 and for 1960-80 respectively give the figures set out in Table II for outputs on various assumptions.

The estimates preferred by the Unesco mission are C_2 for 1960-66 and B1 for 1960-80 (printed in italics).

TABLE 8.2

Average Annual Outputs on Various Assumptions

Assumption		*Average annual outputs 1960-66* *University graduates*	*1960-66* *Twelfth-grade graduates*	*1960-80* *University graduates*	*1960-80* *Twelfth-grade graduates*
A_1	Constant enrolment rates	2,600	20,000	3,000	29,000
A_3(a)	Seven years' compulsory education by 1980	2,600	20,000	(3,500)	(44,000)
B_1	Occupation shift, 1960 educational attainment	—	—	3,459	44,875
C_2	Economic trends upgraded	2,256	42,362		
D_1	Occupational demand (selected sectors)	2,567	10,677		

1. Estimate B_1 takes into accunt a possible occupational shift out of agriculture into the modern sector.
2. Estimate C_2 is based on possible labour-force demand, assuming the labour force in each economic sector has an educational attainment upgraded by 2 percent per annum.
3. Estimate D_1 is built up by occupation, in occupations other than agriculture, fisheries, forestry, mining and construction. It includes manufacture, trrade, transport, communications, power and services.

It will be seen that the estimates for university graduates, averaged at 2,500 for 1960-66 and 3,500 for 1960-80, are markedly lower than the Category I estimates above. Secondly, that the estimates for twelfth-grade graduates are considerably higher in all cases and nearly three times as high for estimate C_2, which is that preferred by the Unesco mission. There are, however, two strange points about these estimates for an average output of 42,000 twelfth-grade graduates in 1960-66 and 44,875 in 1960-80. In the first place, the rate of increase in 1970-80 is strangely low; in the second place, the proportion of twelfth-grade to university graduates is extremely high—over 10 to 1. It is highly unusual for the proportion of technicians to graduates to rise above 5 or 6 to 1 in a country with Thailand's economic shape, where a figure of 4 to 1 or even less might have been expected. In 1962 the actual outputs from MS 5 (twelfth grade) were about 12,000,against 2,800 university degrees—a proportion of just over 4 to 1.

There is, I believe, a simple explanation of these high twelfth-grade figures. They were obtained by estimating labour force increases by industrial sectors and then making the assumption that the educational attainment in these sectors, over the whole kingdom, would be the same as those for the same sectors in the Bangkok-Thonburi area. But this is very far indeed from being true, since there is an extremely heavy concentration of highly educated manpower in Bangkok-Thonburi: 52 per cent of all those with some college education are in Bangkok-Thonburi, and 60 per cent of those with four or more years of college education, with a population into of roughly 3 million in Bangkok-Thonburi to 27 million for the whole kingdom. The table below shows actual educational attainment of the whole population (15+) against what it would have been if the whole population had had the same level of attainment as that of Bangkok-Thonburi. The latter figure is described as 'derived'.

	Actual 1960	*Derived 1960*	*Ratio: actual-derived %*
Pratom V-VII	420,000	1,183,000	36

MS 1-5	619,000	2,367,000	26
College	95,000	736,000	13

This comparison by the whole population over-emphasizes the difference, since the occupational pattern of the labour force in Bangkok-Thonburi is different. But when the comparison is made, assuming that the whole kingdom has the same educational attainment in each occupations as that for occupations in Bangkok-Thonburi, the actual/derived ratio is as follows:

	Actual 1960	*Derived 1960*	*Ratio: actual-derived* %
Pratom V-VII	420,000	879,000	48
MS 1-5	619,000	1,191,000	52
College	95,000	263,300	36

It is clear that the use of the Bangkok-Thonburi ratio must have greatly inflated the suggested educational attainment of the labour force. While the proportions are more widely different for college than for secondary graduates, in fact it is probably the secondary figure which is more out of line. For graduate employment is in fact likely to be mainly in Bangkok-Thonburi, and the use of the Bangkok ratio for them is therefore more plausible. But employment of secondary graduates is widely spread throughout the kingdom, and a 'whole kingdom' ratio applied to it would reduce the estimated requirements of 40,000 by nearly a half.

It is perhaps significant that the estimate by occupational sectors (D_1) which covers occupations accounting for 57 per cent of national income, and in particular almost all occupations which normally require a higher percentage of graduates (government, industry and commerce, as against agriculture), shows a requirement of only 10,677 twelfth-grade graduates in the 1960-66 period, but virtually the same number of university graduates. It may also be significant that the purely educational estimate A_1, which is made without reference to employment opportunity, gives a figure of 20,000 grade 12 graduates for the 1960-66 period and 29,000 for 1960-89—higher than the D_1 estimate even if the latter were rounded to cover all occupations. These two facts together, with the additional pointer that there is considerable unemployment among secondary graduates, suggest that the purely educational estimates are in fact outrunning rather than falling short of employment opportunity.

I have only loaded this report with these somewhat complex calculations because a vitally important point of policy is at stake—whether to aim at an output of 40,000 twelfth-grade graduates in the immediate future or at one of 20,000. In my view the economic manpower requirements do not justify rapid expansion of secondary output beyond a figure of 21,000 to 22,000 per annum as an average up to 1970, allowing 15,000 for post-secondary training and 6,000-7,000 for university entrance. I would justify and describe this as follows, from the facts given above.

By 1960 Thailand had accumulated a large stock of men with some college or secondary education. But a considerable proportion of them were not economically active, and a very high proportion had not completed a university degree or the twelfth year of secondary education: only 27,000 had had four years in college, against 95,000 with some college education; only 109,000 had reached MS 4 or 5 out of 619,000 with some secondary (MS 1-5) education. Analysis of Category I and Category II jobs suggested employment opportunity for about 30,000 college graduates and 70,000 secondary graduates in occupations for which these levels of education might be regarded as highly desirable, if not essential. There was also evidence that quite large numbers of secondary graduates were failing to find employment. By 1961 the Labour Division of the Ministry of Public Welfare discovered from a sample survey of vocational and professional graduate employment that almost 40 per cent of graduates from these levels of education were unemployed and looking for work. If any other evidence were needed for over-production, it is enough to state that in 1963 three of four clerical vacancies in the Civil Service would attract over 1,000 applicants, all with some secondary education and some with several years in college.

Against this evidence of unemployment must be set evidence from industrial employers of a shortage of certain well-trained professionals and technicians, notably engineers and chemists, technicians and working foremen.

The conclusions seem to be:

1. That by 1960 the Thailand educational system was over-producing from its secondary institutions in terms of employment opportunity in the labour force at levels requiring secondary education.
2. That even out of this large production, too small a number were achieving the quality and receiving the practical training which would make them acceptable to industrial employers.
3. That, in consequence, the economic manpower requirements lead to only a modest expansion, perhaps an output of 20,000 or so twelfth-grade graduates per annum, rather than 40,000 (the latter figure having probably arisen from a projection of Bangkok-Thonburi attainments to cover the whole country's labour force). This conclusion is supported by a normal projection of the Category I and Category II posts in a ratio of twice and three times the rate of

economic growth respectively, and by the Thai-USOM projection (D_1) for expansion in specific occupations over that section of the economy where graduate skills are needed in large numbers. The latter shows a lower figure than my own.

4. That, although this expansion should be moderate in terms of general education, a very considerable increase is needed in practical post-secondary training, so that these graduates are fitted to work in the modern sector of the economy and are acceptable to employers.
5. These arguments are expressed in terms of employment opportunity. They are not arguments against higher production of secondary and university graduates simply to satisfy the wish for higher education and to provide an even larger pool of educated men and women in Thailand. This policy could have its own justification, balanced against the necessary investment and possible anxieties about graduate unemployment. What is important is that the larger outputs should not be regarded as essential on economic manpower grounds.
6. That the following manpower targets would be appropriate:

Category	*Stock 1960*	*Wastage to 1970 (40%)*	*Growth to 1970*		*Require-ment*	*Annual require-ment*
I	30,000	12,000	30,000	(100 %)	42,000	4,200
II	70,000	28,000	126,000	(180 %)	154,000	15,400
I	60,000	12,000	24,000	(40 %)	36,000	7,000
II	196,000	39,000	117,000	(60 %)	156,000	31,000

I have slightly reduced the rate of growth for university graduates, to conform to other estimates, and also the rate of economic growth 1970-75 to 4 percent annum, since there is likely to be some slowing down after the spirt in which Thailand is at present engaged. A ratio of 4 : 1, secondary to university graduate, rising slowly to 4.5:1 is retained throughout. The final 'stock' figures for 1975 would give a ratio of 0.9 per cent high-level manpower to total population in 1975.

It is important to note that the annual requirements for secondary graduates are additional to university entry—i.e., students available for on-training at additional to university entry—i.e., students available for on-training at post-secondary level for Category II jobs. Total outputs from secondary would therefore have to be a little over 20,000 in 1962-70 and 40,000 in 1970-75.

In terms of feasibility, and of other projections, these suggestions seem reasonable for secondary graduates. Certainly 20,000 per annum is possible in 1965-70. For 1970—75, the Department of Secondary Education estimated 32,000 in grade 12 (MS 5) in 1971. Other estimates and projections range up to 50,000 (Thai-USOM Projection III).

However, the suggested university outputs are a good feal higher. They Unesco Advisory Team for Educational Planning projected a university enrollment of 28,300 (intermediate) or 38,000 (maximum) by 1975; 21,200 (intermediate) or 23,800 (maximum) by 1970.

These figures, with great deference, seem to me very low in comparison with those for the numbers of grade 12. If there are over 30,000 in grade 12 in 1970, it seems unreasonable to assume that less than one third—10,000—will enter the university in 1970-71, and such an entry, rising a little each year, should ansure a total enrollment of 40,000 by 1975, and an output of at least 6,000, even if 40 per cent fall by the wayside (4,000 out of 10,000 entrants).

Category I need not consist 100 per cent of university graduates. Particularly in top management of industry it is most unlikely to do so. But in most developing countries, where educational qualifications are easier to find than long experience, the percentage is likely to be about 80 per cent. I would be inclined to adhere to a figure of 7,000 per annum Category I recruits by 1975, consisting of 5,500 university graduates and 1,500 from higher technical and other sources. The attainment of a stock of nearly 1 per cent high-level manpower to population by that date seems to be the least which Thailand should attempt.

SPECIAL MANPOWER REQUIREMENTS

Agriculture

That there is room for great increases in productivity and much diversification of crops in Thailand is not questioned. There is, however, little agreement on the best method of achieving this. Some observers believe that, since the agricultural advisory and extension service has been somewhat ineffective, it would be useless to multiply numbers, and that the Chinese middleman is the most effective agent in introducing new crops and methods to the farmers from whom he buys. However, it is scarcely acceptable that a country so dependent on agriculture and so well endowed with secondary and university education should be unable to train and administer a full-scale and efficient system of agricultural advice and extension work, well backed by methodical research. To create such a force is the target underlying the following notes.

At first sight, Thailand appears to possess the necessary educational equipment to create a proper service. Table 8.3 shows enrolments at Kasetsart University in 1962.

TABLE 8.3

Kasetsart University Enrollments, 1962

Subject	*Associate*[1]	*Bachelor*	*Master*
Agriculture	903	330	16
Economics and co-operatives	314	125	22
Fisheries	93	32	—
Forestry	223	99	93
Veterinary	86 (Pre-vet.)	—	—
Irrigation engineering	187	70	—
	1,806	656	131
Grand Total		2593	

1. The 'associate' course is for two years in the university. The bachelor course is for five years.

In 1961-62, 318 students were in their fifth years, 13 (veterinary) in years 6 and 39 were post-graduate students. Kasetsart gave 220 bachelor and veterinary degrees in 1961, plus 256 'associate' certificates.

If the agricultural advisory, extension and research services are put at a somewhat higher figure than those for Burma (since Thailand can both afford to produce more and has the facilities), a structure on the lines of Table 8.4 might be appropriate.

TABLE 8.4

Field Force (advisory/extension)

Sector	*Graduate*	*Diploma*	*Third level*
Agriculture	400	1,000	4,000
Veterinary	200	400	
Forestry	75	150	2,000
Fishery	50	75	

Co-operatives	25	75	
Total	750	1,700	6,000

1. Just over 1: 1,000 agricultural families.

In addition to this field force, it could be assumed that about three times the number of graduates, many from the biological and physical sciences—not from agricultural courses—would be needed for research and for teaching in university and diploma-level institutions—say 2,000. A number of diploma-level assistants would also be needed in research stations. The total force engaged, and outputs per annum to maintain such a force (assuming a working life of 25 years) would be as shown in Table 8.5

TABLE 8.5

Agricultural Services: Total Force and Outputs Required

Service	*University graduate* *Stock*	*Annual output*	*Diploma-level* *Stock*	*Annual output*
Field force (all subjects)	750	30	1,700	
Research, teaching, ancillary	2,000	80	500	88
Total	2,750	110	2,200	88

About 500 staff are already employed in research and experimental stations. In addition, maintenance of 6,000 third-level field workers would involve an annual output of 240.

Kasetsart University is already producing an annual output of more than double these numbers at both levels. Moreover, the Maejoh College near Chiengmai should be able to produce 40 students per annum on its five-year technical course and over 100 from its shorter (higher vocational) three-year courses. Underlying the college courses there are the agricultural vocational schools. It is thus quite clear that in terms of annual output the existing institutions in Thailand could well produce enough raw material at all levels.

Many observers in Thailand agreed that the agricultural service is in fact neither so well recruited nor so effective as it could be for two basic reasons. First, the university training—and probably that at lower levels—is not sufficiently practical. It is most unfortunate that the main university training should be virtually all in Bangkok, attracting potential field staff to a city which they are unwilling to leave, and too divorced from the real agricultural life of Thailand. Even at Maejoh, equipment was far below good standards for a diploma course (only two tractors were available, one out of order) and teaching staff were inadequate both in number and quality.

The second main reason lies in the organization and direction of research services. Part of this trouble may lie in the separate systems built up by the Rice and Irrigation Departments; part is due to insufficient co-ordiniation and direction of the research programmes and inadequate funds provided for them. It will be necessary, if the Research and Field Services are to become effective, to make a new start in both, with longer and more solid research programmes and an entirely different attitude to training for field work in remote provinces. The establishment of new agricultural faculties at Chiengmai and later at Khonkaen would provide an opportunity for a complete revision of the training and attitudes of graduate and diploma field staff, which would have to be supported by equipment, transport, technical literature and many other facilities which would enable graduate officers to do an effective job. This is essentially a matter of quality, training and equipment not of numbers.

Engineering, Science, Management

Engineering. Chulalongkorn is the only university giving

engineering degrees at the present time, save for the irrigation engineers produced by Kasetsart. About 1,350 students were enrolled in the faculty in 1962-63, plus 62 in the SEATO Graduate School (not all Thai nationals). Students may take a three-year courses leading to associate/diploma level or a four-year courses leading to the bachelor degree. About 120 degrees were granted in 1958, and about 250 were expected in 1963. The new university at Khonkaen is to have a department of technology which will presumably go to full professional standards.

Outside the universities, the higher vocational and technical courses must be taken into account.

Higher vocational. The enrollment in 1961 amounted to 29,000, of whom 10,000 were women. Woodworking, building trades, mechanics, domestic science and commerce accounted for 80 per cent of the students. The course corresponds to grades 11, 12 and 13. There were in 1961 8,796 graduates.

Technical. This course corresponds to university grades 14, 15 and 16. It has a growing enrollment, reaching 4,891 in 1961, and probably nearly 6,000 by 1962. It is concentrated on building construction, auto-mechanics, electricity, radio, and television. There were 1,673 graduates in 1961 and probably over 2,000 by 1963. The Unesco Educational Planning Team made projections suggesting enrollments of about 100,000 in higher vocational and 20,000 in technical by 1970-71. Such numbers, implying annual outputs of 25,000 and 5,000-plus respectively by 1973, would, by themselves, go three-quarters of the way to meeting the requirements of the entire economy for Category II personnel, even if these were put as high as 40,000 per annum.

In terms of numbers, the requirements of Thailand for engineers are extremely hard to estimate, since so much depends upon the growth of manufacturing industry and of the engineering elements in irrigation and power supply (including any new development in the Mekong schemes). There were just over 800 engineers and architects listed in the 1960 census. If Thailand is to reach the level suggested for Malaysia ((smaller, but perhaps more industrialized and with a much higher national income), a stock of 4,000 engineers by 1970 might have been a suitable target. However, even if the stock has been increasing at over 150 per annum, this target cannot be attained from the output of Chulalongkorn University, the irrigation engineers from Kasetsart and any new output which might come from Khonkaen by 1970 at the earliest.

If, over the fifteen years 1960-75, output from Kasetsart (K), Chulalongkorn (C) and later Chiengmai (Ch) and Khonkaen (Kh) could be raised to: 1963, 230 (200 C, 30 K); 1968, 280 (250 C, 30 K); 1970, 310 (250 C, 60 K); 1975, 450 (250 C, 60 K, 40 Ch, and 100 Kh) with appropriately graded intervals, the total produced over fifteen years would be about 4,565. Added to the stock of about 800 in 1960, less 50 per cent wastage, this produces a stock for 1975 of just under 5,000, and an output which continues to raise the stock by about 250 per annum after wastage. This suggestion is made on the basis that Chulalongkorn should not attempt to raise output above 250 per annum; that the Irrigation section in Kasetsart should be raised to an annual output of 60 but diversified into all forms of agricultural engineering; that Chiengmai could make a limited contribution by 1970; and that a full new engineering faculty would be established at Khonkaen.

These outputs would be hard to attain, but they do not give an extravagant force of engineers for the needs of Thailand by 1975. Indeed, if industry were to continue its rapid development and agriculture were to get a fair share of engineers, it would be inadequate. But it should be supplemented by engineers of sub-professional but good quality from the higher technical institutions which should play a decisive part in meeting needs, especially up to 1970.

As in the case of agriculture, a decisive issue in the effective production of engineers will be the practical nature of their course and the opportunities given, if necessary abroad, for two years of engineering practice in workshop or field conditions in order to gain proficiency.

Science. So much has been said of the need to improve the quality of science teaching and to increase the output from science faculties that it would be futile to go over this ground here. It is enough to observe that behind every field officer in agriculture should be an output of a least three scientists, and behind every engineer and industrial chemist probably a similar or large output of four to five physical scientists for the whole range of sciences underlying a more industrialized sector and for teaching. This alone would indicate a need for an output of at least 2,000 graduates per annum in the science faculties, excluding the output of doctors, agricultural officers and engineers.

The new Science Foundation will no doubt greatly help in the training and application of scientific personnel. But the real effort and difficulty will be in starting to build in the universities a far greater and better undergraduate and teaching force. In order to obtain a sense of balance, I might anticipate the later sections by suggesting at this point the balance of output per annum which might be reasonable for a university system by 1975: sciences (supporting agriculture, medicine, industry), 2,000;. arts (including social science), 2,000; medicine (doctors), 500; agriculture, veterinary, forestry, irrigation, fisheries, 100; engineering, all types, 450, education 750; total 5,700.

Even a glance at the range of technology associated with modern industry, a modernized agriculture, and medicine, all of which require a first degree in mathematics, physics, chemistry or the range of biological sciences, will be enough to show that a ratio of at least 3 to 1 between the teaching, research and specialist force and the general practitioner is needed. I emphasize this point because none of the projections suggested a figure of output from the science faculties as such which is in scale with the proposals for engineers, doctors and field agriculturalists. A proportion of 50:50 science/arts is probably to low on the science side. An in the case of Indonesia a tremendous effort to build up the science faculties will be needed if this high target is to be achieved.

Management and in-service training. All developing countries suffer from a shortage of practical training and managerial experience, because the industrial sector is at first too small and too young to give scope for in-service training on an adequate scale. The production of engineers and technicians from colleges does not meet this problems, since they are still equipped only with theoretical knowledge gained outside the realities of industrial life. The establishment of the excellent Productivity Centre in the Ministry of Industry is a great step forward in management training. Every effort to encourage the larger firms to develop apprenticeship and internal technical training will be worth while.

Medical

The census of 1960 showed 2,330 physicians and surgeons, but the Medical Register in 1963 showed 3,783. About 500 are probably abroad, and a number on the register are not practising. It might be reasonable to accept a figure of 2,500 doctors practising in Thailand in 1961—less than 1 : 10,000 population. The distribution is heavily in favour of Bangkok (about 1 : 1,100), whereas it is though that in north-east Thailand the proportion is in the region of 1 : 50,000.

The output of medical degrees was about 200 per annum in 1960 and 250 per annum in 1963. The Thai-USOM Task Force gave projected outputs rising to 375 in 1975 and 450 in 1980. The aggregate outputs suggested were (approximately): 1961-70, 2,500; 1971-75, 1,800; 1975-80, 2,100. Allowing for 40 percent wastage every ten years, these figures would give the following results:

Stock 1961	*Wastage to 1970*	*New output*	*Stock 1976*	*Ratio 1970 (prop. 37.5 m.)*
2,500	1,000	2,500	4,000	1:9,400
Stock 1970	*Wastage to 1975*	*New output*	*Stock 1975*	*Ratio 1975 (prop. 44.6 m.)*
4,000	800	1,800	5,000	1:8,900
Stock 1975	*Wastate to 1980*	*New output*	*Stock 1980*	*Ratio 1980 (p'op. 53.2 m.)*
5,000	1,000	2,100	6,100	1:8,700

If 35 per cent wastage, instead of 40 per cent, per ten years were assumed, the resulting ratios would be only slightly improved.

This is a somewhat leisurely rate of growth, particularly since medicine is a first choice among Thai Students. To achieve a ratio of 1:5,000 by 1980 would require the following annual outputs, allowing only 35 per cent wastage from original stock in each ten-years period in order to give the most favourable picture:

Stock 1961	*Wastage to 1980*	*Stock required 1980*	*Output required*	*Per annum*
2,500	2,700	10,600	10,800	540

It is clear that even by 1980 it will be difficult to reach a 1:5,000 ratio. It will not be possible to produce much more than 2,800 by 1970 even if the suggested outputs up to 1970 were considerably increased; and this would leave 8,000 to produce in the decade 1970-80. Since population projections vary a good deal by 1980, as do other economic circumstances, it may be more sensible to confine targets, for the time being, to 1975 and to suggest a more moderate, but still stiff target of 1:7,000 by 1975 :

Stock 1961	*Wastage to 1975*	*Stock required 1975*	*Output required*	*Per annum*
2,500	1,575	6,370	5,445	363

This means 2,800 in 1961-70 and 2,645 in 1970-75, i.e., over 500 p.a., in the 1970-75 period. This would certainly involve a fourth medical school, in addition to Bangkok (2) and Chiengmai, to reach an output of over 500 doctors per annum in the mid- 1970's. It may well be that this is beyond the resources of Thailand, taking into account other commitments.

At the sub-professional level, there were in 1960: 147 first-class health centres (with medical officer, sanitarian and midwife); 670 second class health centres (with sanitarian and midwife); 761 midwifery centres (midwife only). The aim is to provide 500-600 first-class health centres.

There were in 1960 about 4,700 trained nurse-midwives; in hospitals the nurse to bed ratio was 1 : 8. The five-years target was to increase the number of trained nurses to 10,500 professional nurses or nurse/midwives, 6,000 midwives, and 3,500 public health nurses, a total of 20,000. The output from training, in 1960, was 450 nurse midwives, 215 midwives, 150 auxiliary nurses, and 25 public health nurses (post-graduate course). It is almost impossible to calculate wastages, often due to marriage, but they are exceptionally high in the nursing profession, probably at least 6 per cent per annum. If this figure is correct, there might well be room for increasing nursing training to at least 800 p.a., and midwife training to 450 p.a.

Teachers

The detail of the very large supply of teachers required for education in Thailand will be dealt with in the main report. I am indebted to the director and staff for Table 8.6 an extremely useful and neat table of the 1961 stock position by type of school and by qualification.

TABLE 8.6

Teachers, 1961

School level	*Degree*	*Higher Certificate*	*Others*	*Total*
Pratom 1-7	408	3,337	109,780	113,525
Secondary 8-12	2,156	6,694	8,609	17,459
Teacher training	1,110	382	224	1,716
Vocational	632	945	3,471	5,048
Total	4,306	11,358	122.084	137,748

In terms of gross numbers, and a loss of 40 per cent over ten years (which is almost certainly too low, as teachers migrate frequently into other occupations if the economy is expanding fast, because pay tends to be higher outside the teaching profession), the requirement simply to replace this force would be 5,500 per annum. It is clear, however, that, in addition to some increase in numbers, the quality of the force in terms of training to higher levels would need to be improved. Again, I am indebted to the Director for two projections based on the minimum and the maximum projections made by the Unesco Advisory Team. These two projections assume, that 1 per cent of teachers in Pratom 1-7 and 40 per cent of teachers in secondary and vocational schools will be degree-holders, and that 9 per cent of teachers in Pratom 1-7 and 50 per cent in secondary and vocational schools will have the Higher Certificate.

TABLE 8.7

Minimum Projection

Educational attainment	*Stock 1961*	*Requirement 1970*	*Net addition*	*Wastage*	*Output*	*Annual rate*	*Total 9 years.*
Degree	3,200	10,850	7,650	1,750	9,400	1,040	
Higher Certificate	11,000	21,650	10,650	4,080	14,730	1,640	
Lower Certificate	122,100	121,500	—	30.450	30,450	3,380	6,060

On the basis of the maximum projection, the annual requirements suggested are 1,970 degree, 2,960. Higher Certificate, and 7,820 Lower Certificate, a total of 12,750. The wastages were calculated as 25 per cent of the average figure between stock 1961 and requirement 1970. For consistency, these figures are easily converted to the rate of 40 percent on original stock over ten years (which I prefer) and the results then are:

	Degree per annum annum	*Higher Certificate per annum*	*Lower Certificate per annum*	*Total per annum*
Minimum	978	1,620	4,890	7,488
Maximum	1,800	2,800	8,820	13,420

There is a considerable degree of unreality about these figures. The projection based on the minimum Unesco projection produces a total annual output of teachers which is a lower average than the 1961 output, which was: degree, 481; Higher Certificate, 1,632; Lower certificate, 5,695; total 7,808. Further, it is only just above the total probable wastage from 137,000 teachers. On the other hand, the higher estimate involves an output of degree graduates at the rate of 1,800 per annum in the decade 1961-70, which is in any case totally impracticable.

To deal first with graduate requirements in a simplified way, it might be assumed that all teachers in MS 4 and 5 and that 50 per cent of teachers in MS 1-3 should be graduate. The Unesco intermediate projection suggests 471,000 pupils in MS 1-3 in 1970 and 57,500 in MS 4 and 5. At a 30:1 pupil/teacher ratio this implies 15,700 teachers for MS 1-3 and 1,920 in MS 4 and 5, and a total of 9,750 graduates. To reach this stock by 1970-71 requires an annual output of 780 on the 40 per cent wastage basis. If the proportion of graduates in MS 1-3 is reduced to 30 per cent, which is not an unreasonable figure, the result becomes 460 per annum. These calculations omit teachers for vocational and teacher-training classes, for which about another 300 graduates per annum might be needed to provide rather less than double their present graduate strength. This suggests a target of 750 graduates per annum—a very steep rise, but a possible target for 1970.

As a provisional suggestion, I would assess a reasonable 1970 target for teacher output per annum as: degree. 750; Higher Certificate, 2,500; Lower Certificate, 7,000; total 10,250.

Conclusion

Thailand in 1960, a country with 82 per cent of population in agricultural pursuits, had accumulated a considerable educated class—nearly 30,000 men and women with four years of college education; nearly 100,000 who had had a touch of college work. Many of these had gained education for education's sake. The economy was not much industrialized or 'modernized' and education was not naturally regarded as a prelude to intensive training for some technical pursuit; if anything, it led to government service for men, private business and social service for women.

The basic strategy of the decade 1960-70 is to give this educated group and its new recruits a more modern, and to some extent technical training, so that, as it grows and spreads, it is also becoming the leadership of a society bent upon industrialization and upon modernizing its agricultural techniques. This involves a considerable depending of the quality of education, a far greater emphasis on science, a wider application of practical training, and a wider distribution of the educated to rural areas. In particular, I must emphasize the very high target for science degrees.

For this reason, the proposals made here do not involve a rapid expansion of total enrolments in 1961-70, but a preparation for more rapid growth in 1970-80. For reasons given, I have adopted the lower estimates for expansion of secondary education (an average of about 15,000 grade 12 graduates per annum for post-secondary training in the late 1960s, plus 6,000 university entrants), which will give time for quality to grow. The suggested expansion of university output, rather higher than other estimates, is based, I believe, both on economic and social need (as the analysis of medical, teaching, engineering and scientific requirements shows) and also upon a belief that 30 per cent of the graduates of MS 5 will demand and should obtain the chance of university education. In briefest summary, the targets here suggested for average annual output are:

	1960-70	*1970-75*
University (80 per cent of Category I)	3,600	5,500
Secondary (100 per cent of Category II)	15,000	31,000
University entry	(6,000)	(10,000)

This assumes a university entrance of about 5,000 in 1963 and of about 9,000 in 1970. Once again, the Category

II outputs are additional to the numbers entering the university.

I have suggested that university output in 1975 would be balanced as follows: science, 2,000; arts, 2,000; medicine (doctors), 500; agriculture, etc., 100; engineering, 450; education 750; total, 5,800. The figure for agriculture looks extremely small in view of the higher priority which it should share with teacher training in the national effort. But the Advisory Service is advisory, and a force of 700-800 good graduate officers in the field, supported by twice that number of diploma-trained men, should be ample for the field work. The massive number of research and specialist staff will be in large part produced, not by the Agriculture Faculty but from the science faculties. It is in the science faculties that heroic action will be needed to expand output.

Finally, the emphasis throughout is not on rapid educational expansion. It is upon training in practical application. It is not upon vocational schools, which are attempting to anticipate training, but upon good schools, in which science as well as other subjects is well taught, followed by in-service of special training.

8

Education in Japan

Since the end of World War II, Japan's higher education has made spectacular progress. In 1946-47, on the eve of the U.S.-sponsored reforms, Japan had 48 institutions of university standard and 113,320 students attending them. With the exception of about 300 women permitted to attend a few graduate departments, the entire student population was male. The highest level women could reach in the national school system was the junior college. However, we should note that the women's junior colleges provided, However, we should note that the women's junior college provided, at its highest levels, several schools for the professional training of women in dentistry and medicine.

The pre-reform universities formed a clear and explicit prestige ranking order; therefore the entrance examinations were desperately competitive. The preference for a "good" university was no mere academic matter. The rank of the university the student succeeded in entering was virtually decisive for his future life chances.

Although the majority of students were registered in the 26 private universities, it was the 19 national universities that were the most highly regarded. With the prestigious imperial universities—of which Tokyo Imperial was the glittering capstone—as their core, these latter provided virtually all of Japan's top leaders in all fields—government, politics, business, journalism, higher education, and to forth.

Postwar Reforms

The U.S. reform brought enormous changes. They were designed primarily to transform a multitrack, elitist system into some approximation expanded of an idealized U.S. system that is, stuygle-tack, open, with enormously "democratic access to higher education." Overnight, the university population doubled and so did the number of universities. women's colleges were upgraded into universities, and Women made their first hesitant appearance on the great prestige campuses hitherto exclusively reserved for men. The university population growth rate has averaged 10-11 percent annually (compounded), just barely keeping up with GNP.

Today Japan has over 1.4 million students distributed in 380 universities, about 22 percent of the 18-21 years old age group, as compared with about 2.5 per cent before the war (1936). The figure places Japan second only to the United States. Even more significant is the figure for men, since their impact on the quality of the future labor force is greater. Over 35 per cent of them are now attending university, and there is every reason to expect this proportion to reach average U.S. levels very soon. This has already happened in senior high school attendance—today over 80 percent—and university attendance cannot be far behind. In the last few years in the metropolis of Tokyo, 80 percent of the boys have been applying for university entrance and 47 percent have been accepted. Thus, university attendance in Japan's advanced urban areas is already at the U.S. level. Although women's attendance has also increased dramatically, women have not been an enthusiastic about going to university as men. Women still constitute only about 18 percent of the total university population. (If we count the junior colleges, where they are overwhelmingly in the majority, the proportion rises to almost 30 percent.

In a sense, therefore, the success to the U.S.-inspired reforms is undeniable. But through the operation of the same historical irony that is afflicting all the advanced industrial societies, Japan's very success has created vast new problems. We can see the ambiguity of this success very clearly in the student revolt. In Japan, the current phase started earlier, involved more universities and students, and lasted longer than anywhere else. Paris and Columbia University exploded in April-May of 1968, but Tokyo University's medical school had already started exploding in January. The revolt quickly spread from there to all the other faculties, shutting down the university for over a year, and making it impossible, for the first time in its history, to enter a freshman class. By October 1969, the high point, 77 out of 379 universities were in some degree or other of serious conflict, and these 77 included virtually all of Japan's best and most prestigious universities. It was only the rigorous application of the University Normalization Law, which allowed more effective police response, plus student exhaustion that brought peace to the campuses by late/1969 early 1970. Kyoto University, Japan's second most prestigious, was finally able to hold its regular graduation ceremonies for the first time in three years this March.

Japan's universities can be divided into three sectors. Seventy-five national universities with 22 percent of the student population, 33 public universities (that is, those supported by municipal or prefectural, rather than national, governmental entities) with 3.4 percent of the students; and 274 private universities with almost 75 percent of the enrollment. About 15 per cent of all universities can be characterized as religion-related; that is, they are now or have been in the past associated with some religious organization. Most of them are Protestant in origin, and most of them have much higher proportions of women students than the average for the country as a whole. However, there are important Buddhist and Catholic institutions as well, some of them providing specifically for the preparation of priests, some aimed at believers alone, and some offering a non-sectarian curriculum. At various times during the last 100 years Christian schools, particularly those of missionary origin, have had problems with the state or with their own constituencies, but this has not been the case since the end of World War II.

Problems in Higher Education

While the reform solved some historical problems of Japanese higher education—by creating a single-track non-elitist system, eliminating discrimination against women, and vastly increasing access to the university—it did not solve all of them, and it even created new ones. It failed, for example, to destroy the university prestige hierarchy. Although a handful of private universities have improved their ranking slightly and there are minor adjustments here and there, the basic picture is not unlike that of prereform days, although the canvas on which it is drawn is much larger.

At the top of the pyramid we find Tokyo and Kyoto Universities and just below them the 7 other former imperial universities plus a few distinguished national universities. They have the best faculties, the best facilities, the most favorable faculty-student ratios, the best libraries, and the higher budgets in the country. Naturally, they attract the best students. At the next level come the remaining 17 national universities, plus a small handful of private and municipal universities. The next stratum includes the 46 nationally supported prefecture universities plus the better private and municipal universities. And so on down the line.

Because this ranking structure still persists despite the educational reforms, the competitive entrance examination system has become, if anything, even worse than before the war. Before the war only an elite was caught up in this desperate scramble for place; today the numbers who have gone through this experience run into the millions. More than 500,000 young people go through the examination agony every year, and several hundred thousand repeaters go through it twice or more (in 1970 alone, 180,000) spending the time in between cramming at home or in formal schools in preparation for their next chance. (More than one-half fail to make it on their first try). And since boys are more ambitious and attend university in larger numbers, the proportion of the male generation between 18 and 21 years of age that has gone through this examination hell is even higher. In other words, the agony of the elite has been democratized and has now become the agony of the masses.

The postwar university reform was only partially successfull in another area; the elimination of the chair system of organization of faculties, which Japan copied from European models in the late nineteenth century. Although many of the newer—and therefore less prestigious—universities have adopted the U.S.-style department system, the chair system remains if not intact, then only partially modified in the leading national universities.

Financing

While the reform could not eliminate some of these traditional problems but only project them on to a larger canvas, the rapid educational development exacerbated the quality difference between public and private universities. The cost of educational development fell differentially on the public and private sectors. Although the public universities are funded by the national budget, the private universities have carried the brunt of the increased enrollment. Before the war the private universities enrolled about 60 percent of the students (1940 figures), today they enroll almost 75 percent. And this percentage has been going up the past few years.

Since the private universities have virtually no endowments and must depend primarily on student fees, bank loans, and contributions, their average expenditure per student is about one-sixth that of the public sector. At the same time, the average fees per student are over five times as high. Private universities must cover 92 percent of their recurrent expenditures from student fees, as against only 5 percent in the case of the national universities. While national university fees can be held down as a matter of policy because the funds come from the government, the skyrocketing of private university fees has become one of the underlying factors in university unrest.

Until now all proposals for government aid for private education have stumbled over a roadblock written into the Constitution by the American Occupation. According to Article 89, "No public money or other property shall be expended or appropriated for the use, benefit, or maintenance of any religious institution or association, or for any charitable, educational, or benevolent enterprises not under the control of public authority." However, the situation is so desperate to any that Article 89 is being reinterpreted much less restrictively to allow some channeling of public funds to the private universities. Clearly the destruction between private and public is losing its meaning. The higher education of an entire generation can no longer be regarded as a private matters it is a national subject of the highest importance. Since 1970, the government has started to subsidize, through a newly established Private Universities Foundation, 15 percent of the personnel costs of the private universities. By 1974, this figure is scheduled to go up to 50 per cent.

A wide variety of other subsidy plans have been put forward, such as : direct unrestricted grants, a flat sum per student entitled non-interest long-term private bank loans to students, subsidization of student tuition fees, payment for specific services, subsidies for the maintenance of expensive facilities (such as laboratories, medical schools, and so forth). Increased government aid will probably use some of these methods.

Although the government is likely to provide most of the funding, private contributions will also have to increase by a considerable order of magnitude. Some new kind of institution, perhaps on the order of the general purpose U.S., foundation, will probably have to be created to mobilize the resources of the private sector, particularly from the business world.

If all universities come in the end to be funded by a similar mix of public funds, private contributions, and student fees, then the traditional distinction between public and private will lose its meaning, as seems to be the case in England. Although these prospects are agreeable in certain respects, they stir deep anxieties, whether justifiable or not, about possible government interference and the future of university autonomy.

University Autonomy and the Role of Government

Before the war, the Ministry of Education had far fanning authority, particularly in primary and secondary education. One of the principal objectives of the postwar reform was to encourage local and private initiatives through reducing the centralized authority of the ministry. This policy has been only partially successful. In higher education the ministry's legal authority was always limited by the national universities' strong, prideful tradition of autonomy and by the private universities' independent financial situation. The ministry still has ultimate legal control over private universities through its charactering authority, but in fact they are virtually unfettered except for quality control supervision. Recently, for example, four private universities announced plans for the extension of existing medical facilities or the building of new ones. The Ministry of Education vetoed them on the grounds that they were underfinanced. This degree of action in the public interest scarcely seems a dangerous interference with university autonomy.

Although the national universities are more clearly under the ministry's legal authority, they have such deeply entrenched institutions of self-government that no ministry would lightly undertake to tamper with them. Even the prewar militarist-controlled governments rarely dared interfere with the universities, and when they did so it was usually in a roundabout way. For example, instead of openly stepping in and firing a professor, the government preferred to use backstairs pressure on his colleagues to vote him out so that his dismissal was technically not a violation of university autonomy.

Clearly, then, if the prewar militarist governments had to tread so carefully, the postwar Ministry of Education must be even more cautious. The Japanese national university is, in certain respects, the outstanding example in the world of a university completely run by faculty. Although it must deal with the ministry for its basic budgetary allocation, it is completely autonomous internally. All appointments, promotions, and so forth are made by faculty vote; deans and chairmen are elected by the relevant faculties; the president is elected by the franchised faculty (in a few cases with some students participation); and ultimate formal authority lies with a faculty-elected senate or council of some kind. Although in principle all decisions are subject to ministry approval, the ministry would almost never dare reject them, particularly in the case of the great prestige institutions. When a few years ago the ministry raised the possibility of playing a more active role in the appointment of presidents of newer, less well-established prefectural universities, the outcry was so great that the proposal was immediately withdrawn.

In the private university sector there is a great variety of systems of internal regulation. Some of the better universities have developed traditions of faculty self-government as thorough-going as those of the former imperial universities. Others, however, follow a more U.S., style pattern of a non-faculty board of trustees which appoints the president, who in turn may or may not have extensive control over the appointment of high-ranking university officers. There are some universities in which the board has more the character of a board of directors of a private company than of a body of trustees acting in the public interest, and in these relatively few profit-making institutions faculty autonomy is weak or non-existent.

The danger therefore is not any lack of autonomy on the part of universities and faculties but rather the inability to use that autonomy creatively for innovation, experiment, and the meeting of new challenges. The weakness comes from several sources.

First, the inadequacy of public investment in higher education: although the national universities, and particularly the most prestigious among them, are much better off than the private ones, Japan's average investment in higher education is still lower than that of all the other advanced countries of the world, whether measured by absolute expenditure per student, as a proportion of GNP, or as a proportion of the national budget. Second, the imbalance in resource allocation as between public and private universities: as a recent OECD analysis puts it, the private universities enroll almost eight out of every ten students but receive only four out of every ten yen spent on education. In most private universities fully half the teaching staff is on a part-time basis. Third, regidities in the internal traditions of the university, such as the chair system, low mobility, spheres of influence, colonization, cliquism, faculty imbreeding, fragmentation, and weakness of higher authority.

Need for Co-operation

Japan's endemic education problems, which have been under-scored by the student challenge to the very legitimacy of the university and its authority, call for new systems of co-ordination. There are more interest groups, or publics, involved in the universe of higher education today than ever before: industry, government (including its various conflicting branches), university administrations, senior faculties, junior faculties, researchers, graduate students, undergraduates, parents, the public interests, and so on. Before the war, the co-ordinating mechanisms worked reasonably well. The power of the ministry as the agent of the national commitment to higher education was counterbalanced by the deeply entrenched traditions of university self-regulation. The flow of public expenditure for higher education kept up quite nicely with expanding needs. The private universities, on their side, treasured their independence from government and at the same time contributions and student fees.

Their relatively simple co-ordinating system worked reasonably well until the end of the war. But the U.S.-inspired reforms called for new systems. With the reduction of the authority, as well as the prestige, of the Ministry of Education, other bodies arose to fill one or another stretch of the leadership vacuum. The Japan Science Council, for example, whose organization was inspired by the American Occupation, entered the breach in the field of science and research. Associations for accreditation and university chartering, for private universities, national universities, junior colleges, and so forth were organized, each designed to take over leadership in its own particular sector. Most of them, however, failed to establish preponderant authority and ended up by becoming another pressure group rather than the sole leader of its constituency.

Although the individual universities are justifiably proud of their administrative autonomy vis-a-vis outside authority, this very autonomy has often operated against effective co-operation. Individual faculty, department, or chair autonomy is sometimes so thorough-going that it is difficult to achieve co-operation among the faculties of a single university, much less among universities.

The skyrocketing enrollments and costs have put this entire fragile system under intolerable pressure. Nor is there anything in the offing to suggest that the pressure will slacken. On the contrary, there is every indication that the demand for higher education will continue to rise, very likely toward some version of universal higher education. This means that existing systems of leadership and co-ordination will become even less capable of meeting the demands of the situations than before.

Even within the government, the Ministry of Education is no longer the exclusive representative of the educational constituency. Now that higher education has become a mass phenomenon rather than a limited elite one, it engages the direct attention of all the political parties as well as of many legislative committees. It is clearly of concern to the business community and, if *only* segmentally, to the labor movement, as well, particularly to the powerful Teachers Union. Within government, there is a wide variety of interests, the Ministry of Finance's being obvious and traditional. But since education is so important for the sustained high-level growth of the economy, for technological and managerial innovation, and for the technology import/export balance, we find the government's Science and Technology Agency, the Ministry of International Trade and Industry, the Overseas Technical Co-operation Administration, and many others increasingly involved. The Institute for International Studies and Training (Boeki Daigaku), for example, an innovative experiment in early mid-career executive training in area studies and foreign languages, is a product of the thinking of the Ministry of International Trade and Industry rather than of the Ministry of Education. More important pressure for the improvement of language training comes from the Overseas Technical Co-operation Administration and other government bodies concerned with technical aid and the training of Asian students in Japan's universities, than from the Ministry of Education.

It is clear that some changes are on the way, and there is even general agreement on what the shape of these changes must be—something close to the proposals of the Ministry of Education-appointed Council on Higher Education. These would include the revision of the entrance examination system, financial support for the private universities, a quantum jump in financial aid to students, the development of professional administration within the university, increased mobility among universities, diversification of types of universities and their curricula, increased numbers of high-quality institutions, levelling-up of poorer schools, sharper separation of graduate school and research from general undergraduate education, and more junior faculty and student participation in university governance.

To implement these reforms, new types of co-ordinating systems will have to be created, freer of government than the Ministry of Education, but more capable—because of prestige, ability to articulate the diversity of interests in education, and its non-political character—of exercising genuine leadership. Within the university this will require an autonomy that is not merely passive and defensive but one capable of innovation and compromise. Even though all of these new co-ordinating systems will develop, paradoxically the Ministry of Education will, in certain respects, have to become stronger, rather than weaker. Although it will have less control over the universities, it must become a more effective advocate in the competition for funds as against other claimants on the nation's resources.